4x4/13
9x6/14

P9-BIP-611

COLOUR
confidence
in embroidery

For all of you who provide the inspiration
and the challenge to continue learning and creating

COLOUR
confidence
in embroidery

TRISH BURR

SALLYMILNER
PUBLISHING

First published in 2011 by

Sally Milner Publishing Pty Ltd

734 Woodville Road

Binda NSW 2583 AUSTRALIA

© Trish Burr 2011

Design: Caroline Verity

Editing: Anne Savage

Photography: Trish Burr and Tim Connolly

Illustrations: Wendy Gorton

Printed in China

National Library of Australia Cataloguing-in-Publication entry

Author: Burr, Trish.

Title: Colour confidence in embroidery / Trish Burr.

ISBN: 9781863514262 (hbk.)

Series: Milner craft series

Subjects: Color in design.

                 Embroidery.

                 Color.

                 Design.

Dewey Number: 701.85

10 9 8 7 6 5 4 3 2 1

acknowledgements

No book is produced without many helpers behind the scene and this one was no exception. With thanks to Libby Renney and the staff at Sally Milner Publishing for helping to compile this publication, I think this one challenged us all!

I would like to thank DMC Creative World in South Africa for their generous donation of stranded cotton and to those of you who kindly and freely granted permission for use of artwork or photographs, these are mentioned under the individual projects.

Thank you to my family and friends for your continued support and encouragement in this work. To those of you who sent supportive emails it is much appreciated. I would like to make special mention to my Friday class – Merle, Anne, Rosemary, Roz, Helen, Jen – and to Leslie Ann for your encouragement and valuable feedback.

My special thoughts are with my mother-in-law Sheila, who sadly passed on before this was completed, and always shared a keen interest in my work.

To my husband Simon who shares in all the ups and downs, encourages all my endeavours, and gives me space when the deadline approaches, I could not do this without you! To Mum, Dad, Stacey, Tess and Katie, thanks for everything I love you all.

Red and yellow and pink and green,

Purple and orange and blue.

I can stitch a rainbow, stitch a rainbow,

You can stitch one too!

AFTER ALEKSANDRA LACHUT, 'RAINBOW SONG'

contents

introduction

What is colour?

I asked my eight-year-old daughter this question, and she paused before answering, 'Colour is everything!' What makes children so smart, how come they know so much more than us?

On reflection I realised that colour *is* everything and everywhere, it can affect our mood, making us feel happy or sad, excited or calm. It can't be touched or felt so it must be spiritual, an innate quality that we all include in varying degrees.

It became apparent through my workshops that there was a great need for more awareness of how colour affects our embroidery. Over the years I have witnessed what a difference the right use of colour can make to my embroidery. It can either bring it to life, create interest and give it soul, or make it appear flat and dull. I have discovered that good technique is important to the success of a visually pleasing piece of embroidery – but colour is essential.

Anton Chekhov, the Russian playwright, once said, 'Don't tell me the moon is shining; show me the glint of light on broken glass.'

So I am not going to tell you about colour – I am going to show you by example and illustration how colour can enhance your embroidery. This is based solely on my own experience through trial and error over the years, and not on any preconceived theory.

This book has been three years in the making, mainly due to the immensity of the task, but also, once I had begun work on it, my realisation that colour is actually infinite. No sooner had I completed one set of colour blends than another five came to mind.

Having deliberated over and stitched over 250 combinations, I came to console myself with the thought that most probably I would never have to think up another blend because I would have my own book as a reference!

Remember – if I give you a gift, I no longer have it, you do. However, if I give you an idea then we both have it, and if you share this idea with others then we are developing it, expanding on it, and can watch it grow.

I hope these pages inspire you to learn and accomplish more with colour in your embroidery and in return I will have the pleasure of watching the idea grow! *Trish*

The whole world as we experience it visually, comes to us through the mystic realm of colour.

HANS HOFMANN

what's in this book?

In **Colour Confidence for Embroidery** you will discover the secrets behind creating a visually pleasing piece of embroidery using colour to advantage. You will witness the effect that colour has on your stitching, why some colours blend better than others, and how to bring your embroidery to life by using contrast, light and shadow.

Each aspect is illustrated with examples and includes materials, preparation, technique, tools for selecting colours, how to choose colours and how to put them together.

There are twelve step-by-step projects to best represent each colour group – and I have included the little South African bee-eater birds due to popular request! The thirteenth project, the Sacred Kingfisher, is not based on any specific colour but is included as an inspirational piece.

Possibly the most useful and significant aspect of this book to any stitcher will be the detailed chapter on **Colour Combinations**. This offers an accessible resource of over 175 stitched samples to choose from, all categorised into colour groups with thread keys to refer to for each.

In addition you will find chapters on **Complementary Colours** and **Colour Schemes**. The first illustrates which colours look good together and why, and the second provides numerous schemes for you to choose from when creating schemes for your own projects.

The DMC range of stranded cottons has been used as the basis of demonstration. It is well known to all of us, easily obtainable worldwide, appropriate for this style of embroidery and has an extensive range of colours. Some Anchor shades have been used where the DMC shades were not available.

This book is intended as a supplement to my previous books and does not include detailed information on the technique of long and short stitch, so if you are a beginner or need more information on the stitching methods I recommend you refer to the DVD *The Long & The Short of It* or the book *Beginner's Guide to Needle Painting*, together with any of my previous books.

Although this book is based on needle painting and shaded embroidery, the same principles could be applied to any other surface or decorative embroidery.

MATERIALS & PREPARATION

It is not the form that dictates the colour, but the colour that brings out the form. HANS HOFMANN

threads

DMC STRANDED COTTON is my thread of choice for both long and short stitch and needle painting embroidery. It is easy to work with, blends well, is the right thickness, and the range of colours is broad enough to supply most of our needs. As I mentioned in the introduction I have chosen this range for practical reasons – it is easily obtainable, washable, colourfast and provides enough variation to demonstrate the use of colour for the purpose of this book.

The DMC range is available in 465 shades of solid colour, which are presented on their charts in colour families. We will discuss this further in the section Tools For Selecting Colours.

Each skein of thread comprises 8 metres of six easily divisible strands. I normally use one strand at a time unless indicated differently.

Anchor stranded cotton is an equally good brand that can be used together with DMC threads when a particular shade is not available. Don't be tempted to use cheap no-name brands, which may not be good quality or colourfast.

Other threads suitable for shaded embroidery include Au Ver à Soie d'Alger silks and Needlepoint Inc. silks, both of which come in a vast array of colours. Although these threads are slightly thicker than DMC they are beautiful threads to work with and blend well.

Where fine details are required I use Chinese silk. One strand of this silk is slightly finer than one strand of DMC cotton and can be divided further into very fine strands. The brand that is easiest to obtain and comes in an excellent range of colours is Eterna stranded silk (available online – see Suppliers List). To use this silk pull out one strand at a time, cut into quite short pieces – about 40 cm (15 in) as it is easier to handle this way and use as is. If a very fine line is required, separate the strand with the back of your needle and divide it in half.

If you wish to order the real thing from Beijing in China you can find contact details in the suppliers section. This is the silk that is used for the world-famous Suzhou embroidery, one of the 'Four Famous Embroideries' of China, and is available in about 800 gorgeous shades that are easily split into very fine, strands. I find the dark browns and dirty greys the most useful for adding in details.

Thread direction

There is some truth in the idea that the thread has a nap (weave) and if it changes each time you start another length of thread your work may appear uneven. It is best to use your thread in the same direction each time, if humanly possible. To ensure that you do this, pull out a length of thread from the skein (do not cut it). Separate one strand and free it from the other strands, cut off the length you require and thread the needle. Note which end of the strand you have used – the end closest to the skein or the end furthest from the skein.

Each time you cut a fresh length, make sure to thread the needle with the same end you used in the first place; this way you will always be stitching with the thread in the same direction.

For those of you who have conscientiously bound your thread onto little bobbin cards, try to use the same direction each time, but preferably don't use bobbin cards, keep your threads in the skeins.

I keep my threads in little drawers marked 1, 2, 3, etc., according to each line on the colour chart. When I need a particular colour I can just pull out that drawer, and when I have finished with it I put the skein back into its drawer.

 Lining up two strands of thread

This is an old tip that works well to align two threads so that they lie evenly. Thread both strands through the needle. Insert the tip of your needle (about halfway down the thread length) through both pieces of thread and pull through. This forms an invisible fastening (don't ask me how) but definitely makes the stitching smoother.

fabric

Recommended fabrics include:

Medium weight
fine Irish linen

Medium weight
fine Belgian linen

Medium weight
surface linen

Medium weight
cotton satin

High count
Kona cotton

I HAVE NARROWED my choice of fabric for needle painting embroidery down to two main types – and of course the ultimate is linen. By linen I mean good quality Irish or Belgian linen often referred to as 'church linen', not loose-weave counted linen or furnishing linen. The linen you use should be of medium weight and have a very close weave so that you have numerous options for placing your needle. With a very fine linen I use a backing fabric such as fine batiste cotton that supports the stitching and prevents the threads showing through from the back.

The other fabric which is suitable, and very nice to stitch on, is cotton satin. This is a mix of cotton and satin with a close weave that lends itself well to shaded embroidery. If you are unable to obtain either of these fabrics you can use a good quality, high count quilting cotton such as Kona.

To make it easier for you I have listed online suppliers of fabric who sell pieces and/or by the metre.

Fabric colour

I tend to play it safe by using white, off-white, cream or natural coloured fabrics, but backgrounds of other colours can result in different effects on your embroidery.

Below are some examples of the results of using different coloured backgrounds for the same embroidery.

Dyeing embroidery fabric

Church linen normally comes in quite a stark white colour – but you can easily dye it to achieve an off-white or vanilla shade using this technique:

- Add two tablespoons good quality instant coffee to approximately one litre (4 cups) of boiling water in a glass or porcelain mixing bowl. Stir until completely dissolved.
- Add a bit of cold water so it is hot but not boiling.
- Soak linen fabric in the mixture for about two minutes.
- Take out and rinse repeatedly in cold water until the water runs clear.
- Roll the linen up in a fluffy towel to remove excess moisture. Iron till dry.

This will achieve a pale vanilla shade. If you want it a bit darker soak for longer; if you want off-white, just dip the fabric in the solution until it is wet through, and remove.

Backing fabric

I sometimes use a fine batiste cotton backing fabric with fine linen to help support the weight of my embroidery. You could also use a lightweight, good quality calico or fine quilting cotton. It is important that you pull threads at right angles and line up the backing and top fabrics exactly before mounting them in the hoop; if you don't get this right you will get terrible puckering.

examples of results using different backgrounds for the same embroidery piece.

care & equipment

Beauty seen is never lost, God's colours all are fast.

JOHN GREENLEAF WHITTIER

Colour fastness

Using silk in small quantities with stranded cotton should present no problem when washing, but please be very careful when using it alone as it is not always colourfast (see washing instructions below). DMC and Anchor stranded cottons are guaranteed to be colourfast but care should always be taken not to leave your embroidery out in direct sunlight.

Washing instructions

When all the stitching is complete wash in tepid water using a mild soap such as Lux soap flakes, or any detergent used for washing baby clothes, and rinse thoroughly until the water runs clear. Roll up the stitched piece in a towel to remove excess moisture and place face down on a fluffy towel. Iron with a medium setting (not too high, especially if using silk threads) on the wrong side of the work till nearly dry.

To prevent colours bleeding when using silk threads, rinse with cold water until the water is clear. Ensure the stitching is completely dry, using a hairdryer if necessary.

Needles

I use Nos 9 and 10 Richard Hemming crewel needles, 9 for two strands and 10 for one strand. There are other brands on the market which are also good, such as DMC, John James and so on, but make sure they are English-made, not the inferior quality brands which are copies of the originals. You could also use a sharp No 10 – this is good for the fine Chinese silk thread.

Frames and hoops

My preference is an artist's four-sided canvas stretcher frame. These can be bought unassembled in various sizes at any good art shop or you can get one made especially for embroidery from Siesta Frames (see suppliers list). I prefer a frame because it does not leave a hoop mark (and I must confess to being lazy about taking my work out the hoop when I am not embroidering).

I do use hoops for smaller projects, but generally one that is much bigger than the motif so that I have plenty of room around the design. To prevent hoop marks you can place another layer of fabric on top of the main fabric, mount them both into the hoop and then cut out an opening to expose the design. The border fabric acts as a shield for your main fabric. If you do use a hoop use a Susan Bates Super Grip hoop and make sure you take your work out when not stitching to prevent hoop marks. These hoops really do grip the fabric tightly and it is imperative that you keep your work drum tight at all times.

Lighting

One of the most important things for this type of work is a good magnifying lamp (see suppliers). It really will make all the difference to your work.

If you can't afford the real thing use a good daylight lamp plus a pair of reader spectacles placed on top of your prescription specs. These are readily available and come in different strengths – 1.5, 1.75, 2.00 magnification – find the one that suits you. Remember to take your prescription specs with you when choosing the reader specs to ensure they fit comfortably on top. (Remember to take off the second pair when you answer the front door, as your visitors will get a terrible fright otherwise!)

Other materials

Scissors: A small sharp pair of embroidery scissors.

Pen and pencil: An HB pencil or a slightly darker 2B is good for transferring the design and adding in details such as direction lines.

A permanent marker pen (Pigma Micron or similar) in size 005 or 01 is also good.

Masking tape (I could not live without this).

preparation

IF NECESSARY, wash your fabric before use to remove marks and wrinkles. If using cotton satin, iron it on a medium setting; for linen use a good hot steamy iron. Linen is very resilient and will take a lot of abuse with washing and ironing.

Find the grain of the fabric by pulling out a thread on two sides of the fabric at right angles; ensure that the grain is lined up before mounting in the hoop or frame.

Transferring the outline

Obtain a copy of your project outline from your local photocopy agency, preferably on tracing paper. Otherwise trace the design from the book onto a piece of tracing paper with a very fine black pen. All outlines are supplied same size.

Place the tracing right side up, either on a light-box or a window pane. Secure in place with masking tape.

Centre the prepared piece of fabric over the design outline and again fix in place with masking tape, making sure it is pulled straight. Then place the hoop over the fabric to make sure the design is in the right place and that you have plenty of fabric around the edges to fit into the hoop.

Trace the design outline onto the fabric with a pencil.

Final preparation

Press the fabric to set the outline. Edge the fabric with a zigzag stitch on your sewing machine or tape with masking tape or fray-stop to prevent fraying. Mount into the hoop or frame, and you are ready to start stitching.

SHADING TECHNIQUES

*I found I could say things with colour and shapes
that I couldn't say any other way – things I had no words for.*
GEORGIA O'KEEFFE

what is shading?

The main stitches used for shading in embroidery are
long & short stitch, french knots, satin stitch and split stitch

WEBSTER'S DICTIONARY defines shading as: 'Graded markings that indicate light or shaded areas in a drawing or painting'. The Merriam-Webster Dictionary defines shading as: 'The marking used within outlines to suggest three dimensionality, shadow, or degrees of light and dark in a picture or drawing'.

So, basically, shading in embroidery is to fill a motif with shades of colour that graduate from light to dark. This gives the stitching a three-dimensional appearance, which is discussed further in the section *What Brings Our Embroidery To Life?*

Stitches for shading

Here are the basic guidelines for the stitches used in shaded embroidery. If you want detailed instructions for any of the techniques I recommend that you either watch the DVD *The Long & The Short of It* or refer to one of my previous books.

LONG & SHORT STITCH

This is the principal stitch used for shading and needle painting embroidery. A motif or picture outline is filled with rows of long and short stitch, each row blending gently into the next.

1. Stitch staggered stitches across the row; these should be full and close together.

2. Stitch the second row in the next shade of thread. Bring the stitches up through the previous stitches and down into the shape as shown. Work each subsequent row as for row two until the shape is filled.

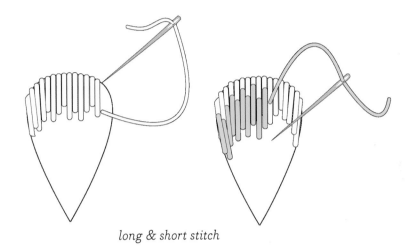

long & short stitch

Tips to achieve smooth blending with long & short stitch

1. Full first row The stitches in the first row must be very full and close together (but not overlapping), so that you have something to work back into on subsequent rows.

2. Come up through the stitches When stitching subsequent rows bring your needle UP through the stitches, NOT DOWN. When you go down into the thread the needle splits the yarn, leaving pock marks or little holes.

3. Splitting the stitches You do not have to split each stitch; you can bleed between stitches as long as the stitches in the previous row are worked closely together. If you come up where there is a gap this will leave holes in your work.

4. Relaxed stitches Vary the length of your stitches in each row and alter the placement to create a natural look. You can go right back into the previous row with some of your stitches and bring others forward, thus preventing rigid rows of colour change.

5. Good direction Stay in line with your direction lines so that the stitches flow in the right direction. Try to keep your stitches parallel to each other; stitches that deviate will make your work look rough and uneven.

6. Think staggered satin stitch.

FRENCH KNOTS

These can be used very effectively when worked in staggered rows of different shades to fill a motif. French knots add texture and interest to a subject.

1. Bring the needle up through the fabric. Wrap the thread around the needle once or twice, depending on how big you want the knot.

2. Insert the needle tip into the fabric very close to the original hole but not in the same hole.

3. Pull the thread gently but firmly to form the knot against the fabric, then pull the needle through to the back of the fabric to complete the stitch.

french knots

SATIN STITCH

Padded satin stitch is used to fill small motifs in needle painting. You can also use the padding underneath long and short stitch to raise an area.

1. Fill the area with straight stitches at right angles to the final stitching.

2. Work satin stitch or long and short stitch on top of this padding. (The long and short padding would be in the opposite direction).

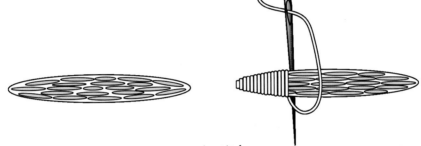

satin stitch

SPLIT STITCH

This is a versatile and useful stitch. When worked in adjacent rows to fill a motif it can be successfully used to shade; in fact, when done in rows it looks like small long and short stitches. I use it a lot for filling stems and branches and small details.

1. This is worked like backstitch except that you go back about two-thirds into the previous stitch.

2. Rows of split stitch worked next to each other to fill a motif.

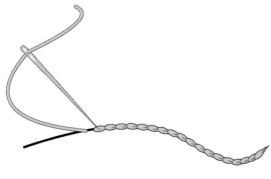

satin stitch

How does colour affect technique?

Is it necessary to stitch perfect long and short stitch to obtain a smooth blending of shades? It is certainly important to try and perfect your technique but it is my experience that the right blend of colours contributes enormously to the visual smoothness of our shading.

The reasons for this are scientific but worth understanding because the direction of our stitching, the colours we use and the texture of our stitch definitely have an effect on our embroidery. Let me try and explain this in simple terms.

REFLECTED LIGHT

Smooth surfaces reflect more light and rough surfaces less light. Therefore, silk reflects a lot of light, whereas wool has a rougher surface and absorbs more light. Have you ever noticed how much easier it is to shade with wool than silk? This is because the rougher wool fibres do not show little imperfections. In the same way different colours reflect light differently. Bright or light colours reflect more light whereas dark colours reflect very little light.

STITCH TEXTURE

A motif filled with satin stitch will reflect more light than a motif filled with French knots. Satin stitch is smoother than the rough surface of French knots, which absorb more light.

STITCH DIRECTION

The direction of the stitching also contributes to slight variations in colour because the lie of the stitch will reflect light at different angles.

1. *Satin stitch at an angle in silk*
2. *Horizontal satin stitch in silk*
3. *Vertical satin stitch in silk*
4. *Vertical satin stitch in cotton*
5. *Vertical satin stitch in wool*
6. *French knots in cotton*
7. *Vertical satin stitch in white cotton*
8. *Vertical satin stitch in dark green cotton*

The little exercise below demonstrates these
theories. The first six motifs (left to right
across) are stitched using the same shade of
green, and the last two in white and dark green.

Below the same six motifs have been rotated to
show the light at a different angle. Can you see
how the colour varies in each one according to
the angle that the light hits the motif? Notice
how much more light the white reflects than
the dark green, and how the colour varies in the
satin stitch and French knots.

Smoother shading

This could be the reason why some of our
shading seems smoother than others. Have you
ever noticed how difficult it is to achieve smooth
shading with white? I believe this is because
each white stitch reflects its own light and
shadow so the overall stitching appears uneven,
whereas darker stitches absorb more light so
appear smoother or flatter.

Look again at the example of the white and
dark green motif to see if this is the case. I have
enlarged this picture so that you can easily see
that the white stitches are more obvious than
the dark green.

This does not mean we need to avoid light
colours in our shading, but if we use shades that
contain a tint of colour, such as off-white rather
than stark white, it will make our shading
appear smoother.

*white and dark
stitch comparison*

To summarise:

- Silk and cotton reflect
  more light than wool.

- Satin stitch reflects more
  light than French knots.

- The direction of your
  stitching creates variation
  in colour tone.

- Light/bright colours
  reflect more light than
  dark colours, which
  contributes to the illusion
  of smoothness in our
  stitching.

TOOLS FOR SELECTING COLOURS

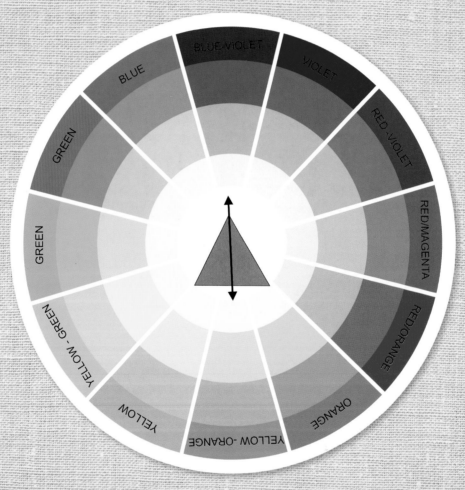

Why do two colours, put one next to the other, sing?
Can one really explain this? No. Just as one
can never learn how to paint. PABLO PICASSO

HOW DO WE know which colours to select? Do we go out and buy a basic set of blue, green, yellow, purple and red because we like those colours?

No, because we would end up with a drawer full of colours that we can't use! We are not alone when choosing colours; we have tools that help us decide, such as a shade chart and a colour wheel.

Shade charts

Shade charts such as the DMC charts reproduced here give us all the available colour options.

6	7	8	9	10
840	159	828	964	955
839	160	3761	959	954
838	161	519	958	913
700	3756	518	3812	912
809	775	3760 (806)	3851	911
799	3841	517	943	910
798	3325	3842	3850	909
797	3755	311	993	3818
796	334	747	992	369
820	322	3766	3814	368
162	312	807	991	320
827	803	3765	966	367
813	336	3811	564	319
826	823	598	563	890
825	939	597	562	164
824	3753	3810	505	989
996	3752	3809	3817	988
3843	932	3808	3816	987
995	931	928	163	986
3846	930	927	3815	772
3845	3750	926	561	3348
3844		3768	3813 (504)	3347
		924	503	3346
		3849	502	3345
		3848	501	895
		3847	500	

16	17	18	19
3827	453	B5200	3072
977	452	BLANC	648
976	451	3865	647
3826	3861	ECRU	646
975	3860	822	645
948	779	644	844
754	712	642	762
3771	739	640	415
758	738	3787	318
3778	437	3021	414
356	436	3024	168
3830	435	3023	169
355	434	3022	317
3777	433	535	413
3779	801	3033	3799
3859	898	3782	310
3858	938	3032	
3857	3371	3790	
3774	543	3781	
950	3864	3866	
3064	3863	842	
407 (3773)	3862	841	
3772	3031	840	
632		839	
		838	

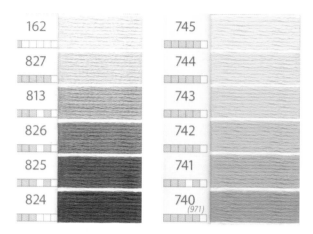

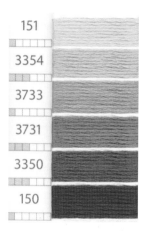

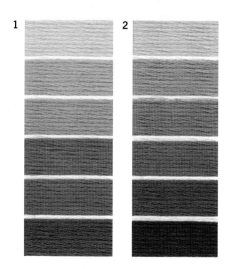

On a visit to the DMC factory in Mulhouse in France I became aware of how significant a task the person responsible for the thread colouring has. It could only be carried out by an expert, and includes dying and coordinating the colours that we see on our chart. Of course this person must have an innate colour sense, and we can rest assured that the groups of colours that we see on the charts have been expertly compiled on our behalf.

The colour families on the chart are a safe option which we know will blend well together; however, to bring more life and interest into our design we can combine shades from different colour families. Here is an example of combining shades from different families:

1. The shades on the left are from the green colour family – 472, 471, 470, 469, 937, 936.

2. The shades on the right are a combination of shades from different families – 3013, 3012, 580, 937, 936, 934.

It goes without saying that a shade chart is an essential part of our embroidery stash – not something you want but something you need and definitely worth the investment!

Colour wheel

A colour wheel, although not essential, can be very useful in helping us decide which colours go well together.

The colour wheel can be used in conjunction with a shade chart. It shows us the main colours available and gives options for the following:

1. *One-colour scheme* – using shades of one colour.

2. *Two-colour scheme* – using any two colours that are directly opposite on the wheel. These colours are complementary, or in other words look good together; when placed together they enhance each other.

Here is an example of red and its complementary opposite green.

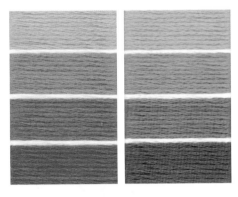

Look closely at this second example. Note how the orange looks more vibrant when placed with its complementary opposite blue than it does next to the yellow.

*Here are four related colours –
blue-violet, blue, blue-green and green.*

3. *Multi-colour schemes* – using the main colour and the two colours on each side of its complement. These are split complementary schemes and can be useful for embroideries using more than two colours. Here is an example using red and its split complementaries yellow-green and blue-green.

4. *Related colour schemes* – using any three to five shades of colour that are neighbours on the wheel. These can be very effective and soothing, especially when used in decorative embroidery.

You can find more specific examples of this in the section **Complementary Colours.**

Colour terms

Here are some of the terms used to describe colour.

SHADE Gradations or varying degrees of a particular colour, such as light to dark, or pale to stronger.

TONE A gradation of colour such as light tones, mid-tones or dark tones. These can also be cool or warm tones.

VALUE The luminosity of colour – more value = brighter; less value = duller

HUE Another name for colour, such as 'it has a red hue' or 'it has a green hue'.

COLOUR BLENDS Put simply, a blend of colour for shaded embroidery includes shades and tones of colour from light to dark. The middle section of the blend is the true colour and the lighter and darker sections are shades of this on either side.

We can also use different values, for example, bright blue, soft blue, dull blue and so on, within our shading. There is more information on this in **What Brings Our Embroidery To Life?**

Selecting colours

Choosing colours also depends on your subject. If you are stitching a needle painting picture from a painting or photograph, you probably want to reproduce the colours as closely as possible to the original.

This option takes out a lot of the guesswork as the artist or photographer has already done the work.

If you are stitching a decorative or crewel embroidery piece, then you need to decide for yourself on the colours to use. The best way to do this is to find a picture or textile design that you like and use the colours as a guide. You will find a selection of suggested schemes in the **Colour Schemes.**

TIP If you are unsure about a colour in your reference picture, it helps to isolate it. To do this, cut a small square out of a piece of white paper and place the paper over the picture area so that the colour within the square is detached from the surrounding colours. The white background will immediately make it apparent what the true colour is.

1. Main colours =
*red, green, yellow.
Choose one shade
owf red, green and
yellow from the
chart. Hold them
against the picture.*

2. Select a leaf *and decide
on the shades of green to
use. You could fit in ap-
proximately 4–6 shades
in the leaf space. Choose
shades on either side of the
green that you have chosen
– that is, lighter and darker
shades. The lighter shades
are from the yellow-green
range and they blend into
duller blue-green shades
from another family.*

3. *Lay the skeins on a piece of white paper and
check that the shades blend well. Replace any that
don't look right.*

4. *Continue doing the same for the rose petals, rose
centre and stem.*

*You could use approximately 6–7 shades in the rose
petals. The stem should be a slightly different range
of greens, possibly more golden.*

5. *You can make changes to the shades as you
are stitching.*

Here are some basic guidelines to help you when choosing colours for a project.

1. Pick out the main colours that you see in the reference picture.

2. Choose the closest shades from your colour chart in a range from light to dark.

3. Lay the skeins side by side either on a piece of white paper or on the fabric of your choice. Now look at the neighbouring colour families on the chart and see if you can introduce some other tones that will enhance or add interest to these. You could use the colour wheel to help you decide.

4. Play around with different combinations until you are satisfied. Leave the room, come back in and look at them from a distance – if one shade leaps out at you, replace it.

5. Once you start your stitching the blend will become more apparent. Hold each skein of colour against the previous row of stitching and make sure it looks okay; if you are unsure you can change the shade at this stage.

Here is an example of choosing colours for a painting of a red rose by Pierre-Joseph Redouté.

finished embroidery

1. Main colours =
dark blue, blue-green, yellow-green, old rose pink. Choose the closest shades from the chart.

2. *Find shades on either side of this, that is, lighter and darker, to adapt to your design outline. For example, you could choose at least 4 or 5 shades of the rose pink from cream, pale pink through to a darker shade of old rose.*

3. *You could choose at least 3 or 4 shades of the yellow-green, going through from very pale to medium.*

4. *Again lay your skeins side by side and check that they blend well and that the colours look good together. You should use similar tones of each – for this scheme they would be fairly muted tones.*

5. *Decide where you are going to place the colours and shades in your decorative piece.*

Here is another example of choosing colours for a decorative piece. This could be something like a Jacobean or Elizabethan design or any embroidery pattern. Say, for instance, that I want to put together a scheme using this William Morris print as my inspiration.

You can find more information on shades and tones of colour in **How Colour Affects Our Embroidery** and **What Brings Our Embroidery To Life?**

Choosing colours in a good light

It is important to select your colours in a good light, preferably daylight to ensure you have the correct tones. The yellowish tones of most artificial light sources can alter your perception of thread colours, and many colours will look very different in daylight.

If you must choose colours at night, make sure you do it under a daylight lamp.

'Yes,' I answered you last night;
'No,' this morning, sir, I say:
Colours seen by candle-light
Will not look the same by day.
ELIZABETH BARRETT BROWNING,
The Lady's Yes, 1844

HOW COLOUR AFFECTS
OUR EMBROIDERY

*My choice of colours does not rest on any scientific theory;
it is based on observation, on feeling, on the experience
of my sensibility.* HENRI MATISSE

A red apple isn't red, nor the lemon yellow.
The sky is seldom blue, only when it isn't ... KEITH CROWN

HERE IS A SIMPLE demonstration to illustrate how colour can affect our embroidery.

The first petal is stitched in shades of pink – 819, 963, 3354, 3833, 3832.

In the second petal, changing the first three shades in this blend to peach tones – 948, 967, 760, 3833, 3832 – enhances the pink.

This is discussed in more detail in the next section, **What Brings Our Embroidery To Life?**

Achieving a realistic effect

At the start of a workshop a student proudly showed me her embroidery of agapanthus flowers, stitched in one shade of blue. She remarked that a friend had said she should have used more than one shade of blue. Her reaction was, 'How many shades of blue does she think there are in an agapanthus? We all know there's only one!'

To her surprise we managed to find at least three shades of blue and grey for her flowers, as illustrated here.

The first petal is stitched in one shade of blue, the second is shaded from light to dark blue into grey-brown.

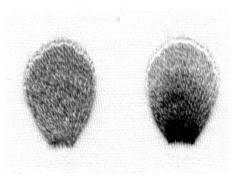

Shades in nature are never uniform in colour. We need to use varying shades to achieve a more natural effect. For example, a leaf could reflect the yellow of the sun or the red of its neighbouring flower petals; it is not just green. Here is an example of leaves stitched in varying shades of green and brown. This creates interest and looks more realistic.

Colour preference and effect

The chairwoman of our guild once described a muted green as 'old lady faded green'. We all have personal colour preferences, obvious from the way we dress or decorate our home, and the colours we favour are quite often the ones we choose for our embroidery. Some of us prefer soft, subtle shades and others vibrant, dramatic shades. (Personally, I like a bit of drama.) Here are some examples of different schemes and the overall effects they produce:

Why do some colours blend better than others?

In her book 18th Century Embroidery Techniques, Gail Marsh suggests: 'Colours should be selected so that they blend into one another without a sudden change in shade of tone'.

In the natural world no colours are discordant, everything has its place and nothing conflicts — that said, the colours will blend better if you use the right shades of tone.

To understand tone better it helps to know a bit about warm and cool colours. Warm colours are the reds, oranges and yellows on one side of the colour wheel; cool colours are the greens, blues and violets on the opposite side of the wheel. Surprisingly, there are warm and cool versions of each.

In essence there are warm, cool and mid variations of colour tones.

antique shades

contemporary shades

soft shades

vibrant shades

If the tones are balanced, you can use almost any colour. JANINE PARSONS

Cool colours

Cool colours are associated with water and sky. Notice they have a blue base whereas the warm colours have more of a yellow base. I like to think of them as 'clean colours' and 'muddy colours', the cools clean and fresh, the warms muddy and earthy.

Yellow-green	Green	Blue-green	Blue	Blue-violet	Violet
772	369	928	162	3747	3747
3348	368	3817	827	341	341
471	988	3816	813	156	340
470	987	3815	322	3807	3746
469	986	501	312	158	333
935	319	500	3750	336	791

Warm colours

These shades are associated with fire and earth.

Red-violet	Red	Red-orange	Orange	Yellow-orange	Yellow
211	3706	967	3856	745	3078
210	3705	3341	722	744	727
209	347	3340	721	743	726
553	816	350	720	742	728
327	815	349	920	741	783
3834	814	347	918	3853	782

Mixed colours

You can have warm and cool versions of each colour, for example warm blues and cool oranges, as shown below.

Cool blue	Warm blue	Cool orange	Warm orange
162	3753	967	3856
827	3752	3824	722
813	932	3341	721
322	3768	3340	720
312	924	946	920
3750	500	900	918

It is not necessary to know exactly which shades are which but, of course, if you use all cool or all warm colours they will blend easily because they are all similar tones.

The colour families on the DMC shade chart show blends of either cool or warm shades but if you use a blend of both it creates more interest. Here is an example in this crewel leaf – the back section is stitched in warm tones and the front in cool tones.

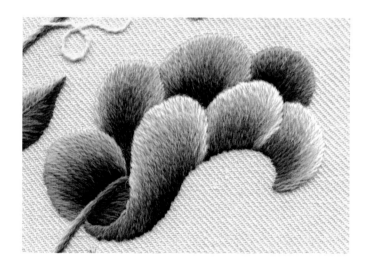

Warm & cool mixing

You can use both warm and cool blends in a combination by using the right mid-tone to marry them up. Here is an example using shades of green.

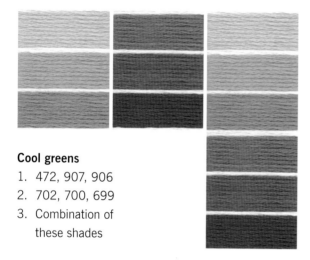

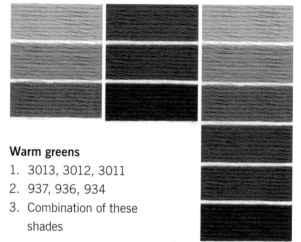

Cool greens
1. 472, 907, 906
2. 702, 700, 699
3. Combination of these shades

Warm greens
1. 3013, 3012, 3011
2. 937, 936, 934
3. Combination of these shades

WARM & COOL GREENS MIXED

I have taken the first three shades from the cool tones and mixed them with the last three shades of the warm tones.

1. Notice in the first example that there is a sudden leap from the cool to warm tones, 564, 563, 562 to 469, 936, 934 – it does not blend well.
2. In the second example by replacing the mid-tone 469 with 987, which has a hint of both tones we can marry up the two colours on either side resulting in a better flow of colour.

You can find more detail on this in **What Brings Our Embroidery To Life?**

Warm and cool greens mixed

44

Mixing colours

You can create different colour effects by mixing shades. This is useful if you can't find a particular shade on your colour chart.

Mixing shades is not as difficult as it sounds — by working alternate stitches next to each other across a row in two different colours you will produce a third shade.

In this embroidery of the iris 'Spartan' I needed a muddy shade of blue-plum in the first row (top of the bud) which was not available on the shade chart. I mixed blue 336 + grey 3799 together to get the right shade.

Balancing tones

It is important to balance the tones in a motif to achieve a harmonious result. If the darker tones outnumber the other tones it will make the finished embroidery look too dark and heavy.

Similarly if the darker tones were too few, the embroidery would end up lacking contrast. A good overall balance would be two light shades, two medium shades and two dark shades.

There are instances where you may need to shade from very light to dark in a small space and will not be able to fit in all the shades — the best way to overcome this is to nearly fill the motif with the light–medium shades and add in the darker shades afterwards.

Here is an example of a flower bud with sepals using four shades of green. The sepals are almost filled with the first two shades of green, then a third is added near the base. The darker green is added afterwards with small straight stitches to create a shadow.

Positioning colours for a balanced effect

It is also important to position colours accurately so as to achieve balance. The lightest shades should be at the top of the embroidery, the strongest shades near the centre and the heavy dark colours at the base so that your motif doesn't look as if it is going to fall over.

For example, the main stem on a flower could be in medium–dark tones with the outer stems and leaves in lighter tones.

When doing a needle painting project based on a painting or photograph you won't need to decide on colour positions because you simply copy the colour placements as they are in the picture. If you are choosing colours for a decorative piece such as Jacobean or crewel embroidery, however, you will need to work out the placements for yourself.

some flower petals with well balanced tones

WHAT BRINGS OUR EMBROIDERY TO LIFE?

Contrasting colour is the best means of capturing and incorporating the dramatic effects of light in a painting.

DESMOND O'HAGAN

contrast in colour

The answer to the question: 'What brings our embroidery to life?' is, without doubt, 'Contrast'.

CONTRAST IS USED to make your embroidery picture more three-dimensional and lifelike by accentuating the light and shadows.

It is not enough to reproduce a good likeness in your picture, you also need contrast in tone. Tone represents the light and darkness in a picture.

Have you ever wondered why the embroidery done by our grandmothers, although pretty, lacked realism? We may think they had fewer shades to work with, but in fact they had as many as we do today – it may be that they did not fully understand contrast.

Without contrast the colours in a picture will lack vitality and look flat and dull. Variations in tone will give three-dimensionality to a two-dimensional picture.

Here is an example to illustrate:
The petal on the left is stitched with three shades of green – 3013, 3012, 3011. There is little contrast between the lightest shade and the darkest shade so the petal looks flat.

The petal on the right is stitched with six shades of green – 3047, 3013, 3012, 3011, 3051, 934. There is a strong contrast between the light and dark shades so the petal comes alive.

How to achieve contrast

Simply put, contrast is provided by using light to dark tints of colour in a motif. Here are three ways to provide contrast in colours.

CONTRAST IN SHADES is simply the difference between the light and dark shades in a picture. Without it our embroidery has no impact. Contrast is probably the most significant way of providing interest in a project. To achieve contrast we need to choose a main colour and lighter or darker shades on either side of it.

This can be done using a light to dark, cool or warm colour, as discussed earlier.

Here is an example of a basic blend using six gradations in shades of turquoise – pale, light, medium light, medium, dark and very dark.

CONTRAST BETWEEN COOL AND WARM COLOURS to provide distinction. Instead of using pale to dark shades we can use shades of cool (clean) or warm (earthy) colours as discussed earlier in **How Colour Affects Our Embroidery.**

This contrast is more vibrant than a light to dark blend and can also be useful if you don't have a lot of space but still want to provide contrast.

There are always a myriad of colour choices that will work in any situation, as long as the tonal value is appropriate.
GAYE ADAMS

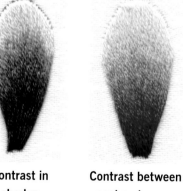

Contrast in shades	Contrast between cool and warm
DMC threads	DMC threads
747	948
3766	353
597	352
3810	351
3809	920
3808	918

CONTRAST IN HUES can be used to change from one colour to the next. You will often come across this when doing a needle painting project – for instance, a leaf may have shades of green going into purple.

Andrew Loomis, a teacher at the Chicago Art Institute, tells us that 'any two colours will be harmonious when one or both contain some of the other'. To shade from one colour into a different colour you need to use suitable mid-tones to marry up the shades so that they merge without any obvious transitions. The mid-tone contains a bit of each colour – here are some examples.

In the first example the shades grade from light chartreuse green into rust. These shades could be found in autumn leaves, or in protea flowers. In the second example the shades grade from light olive green into dull mauves. These shades are found in iris flowers and some leaves.

example one of graduating shades

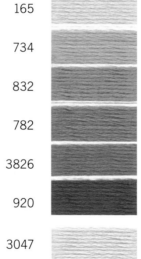

165	**Light tones**
734	**Mid-tones** note how the mid-tone (DMC 782) links up the green-gold in the 832 and the golden rust of the 3826. This is the shade that merges the greens into the rusts without an obvious transition because it contains a hint of each colour.
832	
782	
3826	
920	**Dark tones**

example two of graduating shades

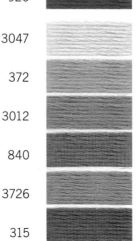

3047	**Light tones**
372	**Mid-tones** note how the mid-tone (DMC 840) links up the green of the 3012 and the mauve of the 3726. It has a hint of both colours in it so merges the greens into the mauves without an obvious transition.
3012	
840	
3726	
315	**Dark tones**

50

three-dimensional effect

I want my paintings to have a light of their own; they must glow from inside ... DOUGLAS PORTWAY

ANY THREE-DIMENSIONAL object has depth, which is what makes it appear lifelike and makes it glow. This is what shading does in needle painting – as the shades blend from one into another the object we are stitching appears radiant, almost luminous. With shading the illusion of three-dimensional reality appears on our fabric – I think this is why shading is so fascinating, for it brings our embroidery to life.

To create a three-dimensional illusion in our embroidery we need to provide the effect of light and shadow on an object.

Lee Hammond illustrates this well in her book Drawing in Colour – Birds. With her permission I am going to use this egg shape to demonstrate the elements of shading which can be found in every three-dimensional shape

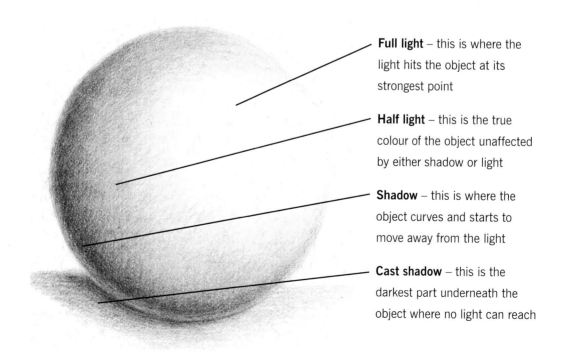

Full light – this is where the light hits the object at its strongest point

Half light – this is the true colour of the object unaffected by either shadow or light

Shadow – this is where the object curves and starts to move away from the light

Cast shadow – this is the darkest part underneath the object where no light can reach

Now let's apply these shading elements to a simple petal motif in long and short stitch shading.

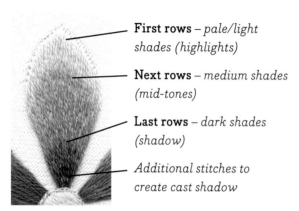

— **First rows** – *pale/light shades (highlights)*

— **Next rows** – *medium shades (mid-tones)*

— **Last rows** – *dark shades (shadow)*

— *Additional stitches to create cast shadow*

Light and shadow

As discussed, light and shadow visually define an object – but how do we know where to place the light and shadow in our picture?

Everything has a light source which provides light in some areas and shadows on the opposite side.

We need to decide where the light source is coming from in our picture and add highlights on this side. The shadows will be on the opposite side. A good rule of thumb is to make the light source on the top left of your design so that everything in that area will appear lighter and everything bottom right will appear darker.

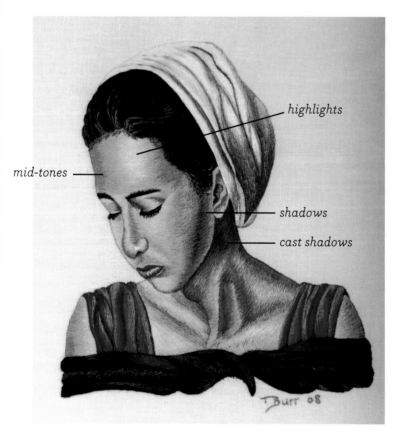

highlights

mid-tones

shadows

cast shadows

In this portrait of Elise the light source is at top left. The light and shadow make her look more lifelike and provide a radiance to her skin.

Using the true shades of light and shadow helps to achieve a more realistic effect. For instance, light shades often reflect the sun (giving them a hint of yellow) and shadow shades are devoid of sunlight (giving them a greyish brown tint). Here are some examples of shades to use for light and shadow from the DMC chart. The first two shades represent highlights and the last two shades shadows.

Shades from the DMC chart to use for light and shadow

1	2	3	4	5	6
819	948	3823	818	712	153
761	353	3855	3689	3770	3609
760	352	3854	3688	225	3608
3712	351	722	3687	224	3607
3830	920	351	3803	3859	718
3858	918	350	3802	632	915

7	8	9	10	11	12
352	892	891	3770	Blanc	3865
351	3801	309	225	762	712
350	666	150	152	3743	225
347	321	777	223	3042	3727
3777	815	814	3722	3041	3688
3857	902	938	3858	3740	3687

Shades from the DMC chart to use for light and shadow

13	14	15	16	17	18
351	3865	Blanc	Blanc	3747	352
350	948	211	819	341	3712
349	353	210	605	160	3832
321	352	209	3806	161	3350
3777	3712	3835	3805	317	3803
3857	3328	3834	917	413	3685

19	20	21	22	23	24
3047	3047	613	729	822	3047
3013	3013	612	3829	3782	372
3012	3012	611	435	3032	3013
3011	829	610	434	640	3012
3051	433	3781	433	3787	3011
3021	300	3021	898	3021	610

making something shine

The colour of the object illuminated partakes of the colour of that which illuminates it. LEONARDO DA VINCI

AS DISCUSSED EARLIER, highlight colours are not pure white but rather a very pale shade of the main colour plus a hint of the reflected colour. Sunlight reflected onto an object would give the colour a hint of yellow whereas a bluish light on a cloudy day would result in a grey tint.

A neighbouring colour could also be reflected in the highlight – for instance, the red from a red rose could be reflected into the green of the leaves. Here are some examples of how to add highlights to a motif:

Notice that the highlights on these three objects all contain a hint of yellow, indicating sunlight.

1. The highlight shades on the red ribbon are peach tones going into red.

2. The shine on the green leaf is pale creamy white going into yellow-green, into green.

3. The highlights on the flower petals are creamy peach going into peach, into burgundy.

creating shadow

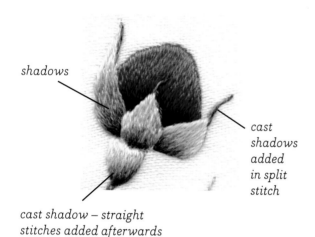

shadows

cast shadows added in split stitch

cast shadow – straight stitches added afterwards

THE DARKER SHADES in a colour blend will give the illusion of shadow but a true shadow colour is obtained by mixing the complementary opposite with the main colour – for instance, red + green = brown. Most shadows will be a grey/brown shade; pure black is rarely used.

I got out my daughter's paint box and mixed these complementary opposites to discover what shades they made and then matched them up to the nearest thread colour. Here are some examples of adding shadow to a motif.

Remember that an object contains both shadow and cast shadow, as demonstrated by the egg example. In embroidery we can blend the shadow shade in with our main shades and the cast shadow can be added in afterwards.

This is done either by blending in a few straight stitches at the base or by adding a line of split stitch. In this way we can add small details when the stitching is complete. Here is an example.

✳ TIP Cast shadows

Cast shadows can be added in when the embroidery is complete to emphasize certain aspects of the picture. This can be done with fine split stitch lines using a very dark shade of brown, grey or a dull shade of the colour used.

56

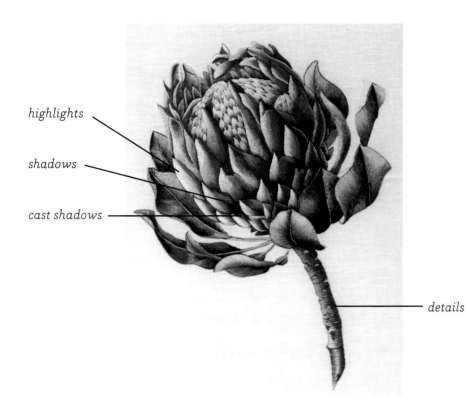

highlights

shadows

cast shadows

details

This needle-painted protea illustrates the use of shadows well. The petals of the protea are shaded from light to dark with shadows at the base, then split stitch outlines have been added in a darker shade for cast shadows.

Notice also the little notches added on the branch, a good example of adding details, as discussed further below.

Here is a simple example of adding a cast shadow to a turnover on a petal.

1. Underline the turnover with split stitch using one strand of the darkest shade.

2. Work straight stitches over the previous stitching towards and over the split stitch line.

adding the details

The details are not the details. They make the design.
CHARLES EAMES

little hairs on the stem and centre of the poppy

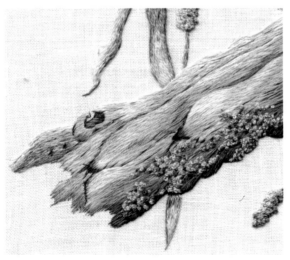

lichen and notches on the branch

ANOTHER WAY to make our embroidery look more realistic is to add details. This could be notches on a branch, hairs on stems, fine wispy bird feathers or shadows and highlights.

Have you ever noticed how when others look at our embroidery they pick out these little details: 'Oh, look at those hairs on the stem – they are so fine' or 'Look at the lichen on the branch – it looks so real' or 'The bird's feathers look so fluffy – how did you do that?'

It is these little details that create interest in our work and make it more artistic.

I add the details afterwards when the main embroidery is complete. You could use one strand of DMC stranded cotton but I like to use Chinese silk thread, the reason being that it can be subdivided or split into very fine strands almost a hair's breadth in width. This gives me carte blanche to add in those delicate details without appearing too heavy.

Here are some examples of details that have been added in once the main stitching is complete:

the wispy side feathers and gold edging on the back of the kingfisher

COLOUR
COMBINATIONS

If you want to colour beautifully, colour as best pleases yourself at quiet times, not so as to catch the eye, nor to look as if it were clever or difficult to colour in that way, but so that the colour be pleasant to you when you are happy, or thoughtful. When you are fatigued or ill-tempered you will not choose them so well. JOHN RUSKIN

choosing combinations

THIS SECTION PROVIDES a helpful resource
to refer to when choosing colour combinations.
There are over 160 blends to choose from, each
being a mix of shades from colour families on
the DMC shade chart.

Each flower symbolises a colour group and each
petal is stitched with six shades of colour from
light to dark – that is, highlights, mid-tones and
shadows. The petals are numbered and each

one corresponds to a list of the DMC stranded
cottons used for easy reference.

Remember that a highlight shade can include
a hint of yellow (from sunlight) so some of the
light shades will appear to have a yellowish tint,
others will just be a paler shade of the main
colour. The shadow shade can be a mix of the
complementary opposite and the main colour or
it could be a deeper shade of the main colour.

✽ Points to remember when choosing combinations
TIP

You can adjust the shades to fit a smaller
or larger motif by adding or removing some of
the shades. When doing this try to avoid any
sudden leaps in tone; use the correct mid-tone
to keep the shades flowing as much as possible.

You can fit more shades into a small motif if you
split right back into each preceding row in your
long and short stitch, or you can decrease the
number of shades and use contrast in hues.

You can increase the amount of shades in a
large motif by adding a paler shade (or off-
white at the beginning and a deeper shadow
shade at the end (browns/greys). Alternatively,
you can stitch more than one row of a shade
to extend the shade range.

When you have chosen all your colours, place
them on a piece of white paper or fabric and
leave them somewhere where you can see
them from a distance when you pass by – if
any colours leap out at you replace them with
a more suitable shade.

The lighter shades should be placed at the
top of the design (lighter) and the darker
shades at the bottom (heavier) so that it
appears balanced.

Try to keep a good balance of shades in a
blend – for example, two light, two medium
and two dark shades, or three light to medium
and three medium to dark.

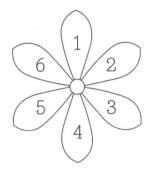

petal numbers guide for DMC *thread keys*

CORAL RED

Of all the hues, reds have the most potency.
Use them to punctuate white, burn into bronzes,
or dynamite black. JACK LENOR LARSEN

1	2	3	4	5	6
819	948	3823	818	712	153
761	353	3855	3689	3770	3609
760	352	3854	3688	225	3608
3712	351	722	3687	224	3607
3830	920	351	3803	3859	718
3858	918	350	3802	632	915

REDS - TERRACOTTA

Oh, I love red. I'm very loyal to my colours.
I love violet. ELIZABETH TAYLOR

1	2	3	4	5	6
351	350	3712	3705	891	3712
3830	347	3328	3801	666	3328
355	816	355	347	321	347
221	221	221	221	498	304
3857	3857	3857	3857	815	815
838	**938**	**938**	**838**	**902**	814

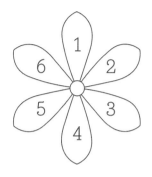

petal numbers guide for DMC *thread keys*

OLD ROSE PINKS

Slow buds the pink dawn like a rose | From out night's gray and cloudy sheath; | Softly and still it grows and grows, | Petal by petal, leaf by leaf.
SUSAN COOLIDGE, 'The Morning Comes Before the Sun'

1	2	3	4	5	6
819	225	3770	3770	819	3770
3713	224	225	225	3779	225
3354	223	224	152	3778	224
3688	3722	223	3859	356	3861
3726	3858	3726	632	3858	3860
315	**3857**	**315**	**898**	**3857**	779

ROSE PINKS

The very pink of perfection.
OLIVER GOLDSMITH

1	2	3	4	5	6
818	225	948	819	818	3713
3326	151	3713	963	3326	761
899	3688	3354	3716	3833	760
335	3687	3733	962	3328	3712
3831	3350	3731	961	355	3722
816	**150**	**3350**	**3722**	**3777**	3721

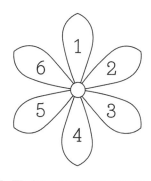

petal numbers guide for DMC *thread keys*

PINKS-MAGENTA

I adore that pink! It's the navy blue of India!
DIANA VREELAND

1	2	3	4	5	6
819	605	963	948	818	3770
963	603	957	967	605	818
605	602	956	957	3806	605
3608	601	601	962	3805	604
3607	326	600	602	3804	603
3804	777	150	3805	326	602

MAUVE-GRAPE

Mauve is just pink trying to be purple.
JAMES WHISTLER

1	2	3	4	5	6
778	151	153	962	153	762
3688	3688	316	3687	3836	3743
3687	3726	315	3803	3835	3042
3803	315	3802	3685	3834	3041
902	3802	902	154	154	3740
938	938	938	3371	3371	838

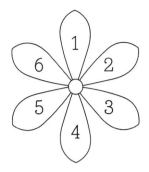

petal numbers guide for DMC *thread keys*

VIOLET-PURPLE

I think it pisses God off if you walk by the colour purple in a field somewhere and don't notice it.
ALICE WALKER

1	2	3	4	5	6
209	3747	211	211	211	153
208	157	155	210	210	554
3837	794	3746	340	209	553
550	793	792	3746	208	327
154	3746	791	333	333	3834
3371	333	823	791	791	154

POWDER BLUE

Blue colour is everlastingly appointed by the Deity to be a source of delight. JOHN RUSKIN

1	2	3	4	5	6
3756	3747	3756	3756	3756	blanc
775	157	162	3753	3753	762
3841	794	827	3840	3752	159
3325	793	813	809	932	160
794	161	334	3839	931	161
793	317	161	161	317	413

65

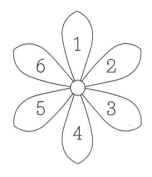

petal numbers guide for DMC *thread keys*

BLUES

Oh! 'darkly, deeply, beautifully blue',
As someone somewhere sings about the sky.
LORD BYRON

1	2	3	4	5	6
828	162	519	3841	162	800
827	3840	518	3755	813	809
813	3839	517	799	826	799
931	3807	311	798	825	312
930	792	823	797	803	336
3750	791	939	791	823	823

TURQUOISE-TEAL

More varied than any landscape was the landscape in
the sky, with islands of gold and silver, peninsulas of
apricot and rose against a background of many shades
of turquoise and azure. CECIL BEATON

1	2	3	4	5	6
747	747	564	828	747	747
964	964	993	598	598	3766
959	993	992	3849	597	807
3814	3851	3848	3848	3809	3809
991	943	3847	3847	3808	924
500	991	500	3808	924	3371

COLOUR COMBINATIONS

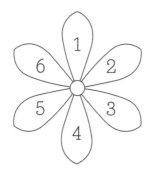

petal numbers guide for DMC *thread keys*

BLUE-GREENS

The sea a dark greenish blue like a fig.
EUGENE DELACROIX

1	2	3	4	5	6
928	3072	369	772	928	369
3817	647	563	955	3813	368
3816	522	562	563	502	320
3815	502	367	562	501	163
561	501	520	561	500	501
500	500	934	500	934	500

GREENS

Green is the prime colour of the world, and that from which its loveliness arises.
PEDRO CALDERON DE LA BARCA

1	2	3	4	5	6
772	472	704	369	907	472
3348	471	703	368	906	471
471	3347	702	320	905	988
470	3346	987	367	904	987
937	3345	3345	3362	3345	986
936	935	935	934	935	319

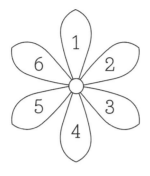

petal numbers guide for DMC *thread keys*

AVOCADO GREEN

They'll sell you thousands of greens. Veronese green and emerald green and cadmium green and any sort of green you like, but that particular green, never.   PABLO PICASSO

1	2	3	4	5	6
3047	772	3013	524	772	3072
3013	472	3364	3013	3348	524
3012	471	3363	3012	3364	3053
3011	470	3362	3011	3363	3052
3051	3346	935	936	3362	3051
3021	3362	934	935	935	3021

OLIVE GREENS

For a warm earthy palette, add raw umber, cadmium red light, burnt umber and olive green.
LISA BUCK-GOLDSTEIN

1	2	3	4	5	6
3047	3047	834	372	165	3047
372	372	832	3012	734	834
3013	370	831	3011	733	833
3012	831	830	936	732	733
3011	830	829	935	730	732
610	869	3781	934	830	730

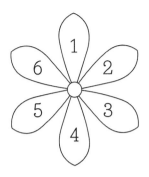

petal numbers guide for DMC *thread keys*

GOLDS

Nature's first green is gold.
ROBERT FROST

1	2	3	4	5	6
746	677	3047	746	677	746
677	676	3046	677	3822	3047
3822	729	834	676	3821	3046
3821	783	833	422	3820	3045
729	782	831	3838	783	167
3829	780	830	420	782	610

YELLOW–SAFFRON

There are painters who transform the sun into a yellow spot, but there are others who, thanks to their art and intelligence, transform a yellow spot into the sun. PABLO PICASSO

1	2	3	4	5	6
746	3078	3078	746	744	746
745	727	727	3078	743	745
744	726	726	727	742	744
743	728	743	743	741	725
729	783	977	742	3853	728
680	782	976	3853	921	783

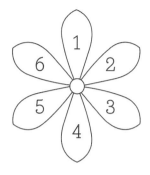

petal numbers guide for DMC *thread keys*

ORANGE/BURNT ORANGE

Orange is the happiest colour.

FRANK SINATRA

1	2	3	4	5	6
3856	3855	3856	977	3825	402
722	3854	402	976	722	3776
721	3853	922	301	922	921
720	921	921	920	921	920
920	920	400	919	920	355
918	918	300	3777	355	3857

GOLDEN BROWN–COPPER

Like warm brown sugar.

TRISH BURR

1	2	3	4	5	6
729	782	783	977	3827	3855
3829	780	782	976	977	3827
435	433	780	3826	976	435
434	898	975	975	434	434
433	938	300	300	433	433
898	3371	3857	3857	898	898

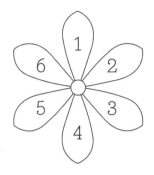

petal numbers guide for DMC *thread keys*

BROWNS

I cannot pretend to feel impartial about colours.
I rejoice with the brilliant ones and am genuinely
sorry for the poor browns.   WINSTON CHURCHILL

1	2	3	4	5	6
613	3866	3770	739	738	543
612	842	950	738	437	3864
611	841	3064	437	436	3863
610	840	3772	3863	434	3862
3781	3781	3860	3862	632	433
3021	3021	779	839	3857	898

GREY-BROWNS

The fundamental grey, which differentiates the
masters, expresses them, is the soul of all colour.
ODILON REDON

1	2	3	4	5	6
822	712	712	746	3072	746
3782	613	739	3047	647	613
3032	3032	612	612	646	642
640	3790	640	610	3787	646
3787	3781	3787	3781	3021	645
3021	3021	3021	3021	3371	844

petal numbers guide for DMC *thread key*

WHITES–NATURALS

White ... is not a mere absence of colour; it is a shining and affirmative thing, as fierce as red, as definite as black ... God paints in many colours; but He never paints so gorgeously, I had almost said so gaudily, as when He paints in white. G. K. CHESTERTON

1	2	3	4	5	6
blanc	blanc	blanc	blanc	blanc	blanc
3865	3865	3865	3865	3865	3865
3770	3866	3866	712	762	712
950	644	3033	613	453	739
3864	524	3782	612	452	738
3863	3022	3790	611	3861	437

72

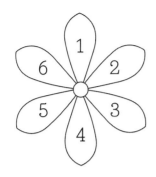

petal numbers guide for DMC *thread key*

PASTELS

Muted, pastel shades that are restful to the eye.

It is still colour, it is not yet light.   PIERRE BONNARD

1	2	3	4	5	6
Soft yellow	Dusty blue	Soft peach	Soft jade	Soft gold	Dusty pink
3865	3865	3865	3865	3865	3865
746	762	3770	928	746	819
3823	3747	967	3813	677	225
745	159	3824	503	3046	778
3855	160	352	926	372	3727
437	317	356	3768	371	3861

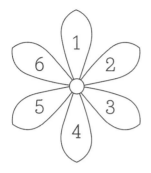

petal numbers guide for DMC *thread key*

VIBRANT

Deep, luminous shades of colour with strong contrasting hues from bright to very dark.

When the colour achieves richness, the form attains its fullness also. PAUL CÉZANNE

1	2	3	4	5	6
Jade	Red	Bronze	Mauve	Periwinkle	Ultramarine
912	304	780	3687	155	996
3851	815	400	3803	3746	3843
3814	3685	300	3834	333	825
3847	154	3857	154	791	803
500	3371	938	3371	336	823
310	310	3371	310	939	310

Clean fresh shades of colour that conjure up images of sun, sea, candy and ripe fruit. These shades are derived from the pure primary colours which accounts for their brightness.

CONTEMPORARY

Purer colours ... have in themselves, independently of the objects they serve to express, a significant action on the feelings of those who look at them. HENRI MATISSE

1	2	3	4	5	6
3078	746	948	818	772	3756
3855	772	967	963	955	747
3825	955	3824	957	954	3761
3341	964	3341	603	913	3325
3705	3766	3705	602	3851	809
3801	807	3801	601	3850	3838

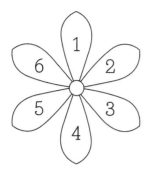

petal numbers guide for DMC *thread key*

ANTIQUE

If time were a colour, I bet it would be a tasteful off-white.

GREG PARRISH

1	2	3	4	5	6
ecru	ecru	822	945	613	712
453	543	524	758	927	3047
3042	225	522	3778	926	3046
3041	224	3022	3830	3768	3045
3740	3859	640	355	930	420
779	632	3781	3857	3799	869

WHEN CHOOSING ANTIQUE shades it helps to understand the historical aspect and the dyes available at that time. Briefly, the thread colours available to women in the seventeenth and eighteenth centuries were china blue, dull marine blue, Jacobean green, olive green, muddy red, terracotta, dull rose pink, wine red, brown and grey.

The dyes available in this period were extracted from plants, vegetables and barks, which could explain why they have a muddy, smoky consistency.

INDIGO The most commonly available dye, derived from the indigo plant (various Indigofera species), and doubtless the reason for a prevalence of blue and white embroidery at this time. According to the degree of tint used, different shades of blue could be achieved.

YELLOW A muddy yellow was derived from the wood of fustic or yellowwood, Moras tinctoria. Saffron was available, but at great expense, and used sparingly to create a purer form of yellow.

GREEN Fustic was mixed with indigo to create olive or pine green. Grey-green was derived from the leaves of the staghorn sumac tree, Rhus typhina, and marine blue from a mix of indigo and fustic.

RED A pure red dye was not obtainable. A muddy red was obtained from the roots of the madder plant, Rubia tinctorum. Mixing it with brown, a terracotta shade could be achieved. It was not until much later that a dye was discovered from the cochineal insect, Dactylopius coccus, which gave us the rich, purer reds we know today.

PINK A pink with an underlying mauve tint was derived from the juice of pokeberries (Phytolacca species), and shades of dull rose pink from madder.

PURPLE A juice extracted from the bark of the logwood tree, Haematoxylum campechianum, and mixed with madder or indigo resulted in mauve or violet.

BROWN AND GREY These colours were derived from the bark of the walnut tree and mixed with fustic to create gold.

*The following artistic combinations illustrate
how you can blend from one colour family into a
completely different set of colours by using the appropriate
mid-tones to blend one shade into another.*

ARTISTIC ONE

These unusual blends are found in nature in leaves, stems, flowers and plants,

*There were apples painted in pale green and bright red on a ground of emerald green leaves.
It is all colour. One might say it was a Cézanne.* MAURICE DENIS

1	2	3	4	5	6
3047	3078	3047	3013	165	3047
3013	165	372	3053	734	834
3012	3819	3012	3052	832	734
829	733	840	611	782	3012
433	831	3726	632	3826	3363
300	869	315	3858	920	520

COLOUR COMBINATIONS

78

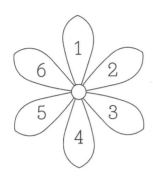

ARTISTIC TWO

These unusual blends of colour are inspired by art and textiles.

I saw a sunset in Queretaro that seemed to reflect the colour of a rose in Bengal.   JORGE LUIS BORGES

1	2	3	4	5	6
951	746	3823	746	746	3823
353	369	3855	3823	3770	3855
3859	3817	3045	3856	3774	3045
3726	926	640	402	452	640
3740	3787	3787	356	451	3768
838	3021	3021	3721	535	924

COMPLEMENTARY COLOURS

All colours are the friends of their neighbours and the lovers of their opposites. MARC CHAGALL

This section illustrates which colours look good together based on basic colour theory and could be useful when choosing colour schemes.

Complementary scheme

The word 'complement' (to go well together, to harmonise) should not be confused with the word 'compliment' (to praise or flatter). The complementary colour is the opposite on the colour wheel and that which best harmonises with the main colour. This scheme looks best when you use a warm colour against a cool colour, such blue versus orange. It is best to choose a dominant colour and use the complementary colours as accents to provide more balance.

Split complementary scheme

The split complementaries are the two colours on either side of the complementary opposite. This scheme offers more variety in colours and will provide a dramatic effect. Again, it is best to use a dominant warm colour against a range of cool colours to put emphasis on the warm colour.

It could be useful when deciding which shades of green to use in the leaves of a red rose, for example. You could use both yellow and blue-green shades to provide more interest against the red of the rose.

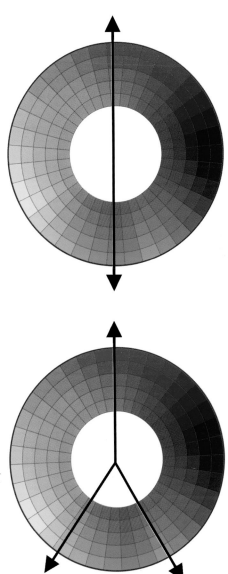

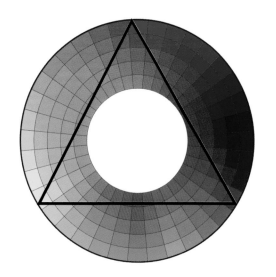

Triadic colour scheme

The triadic scheme uses three colours equally spaced around the wheel in a triangle – it offers high contrast while still retaining harmony and offers more variety of colours. Again, use a dominant colour and the other colours as accents. If the colours look too gaudy, try using more subdued shades. This scheme could be useful when choosing colours for a decorative piece that requires more variety.

It is not important to understand the theory behind these concepts but it is helpful to know why some colours work well together in our embroidery.
On the following pages are examples of colours that work well together for each group using this concept.

CORAL RED

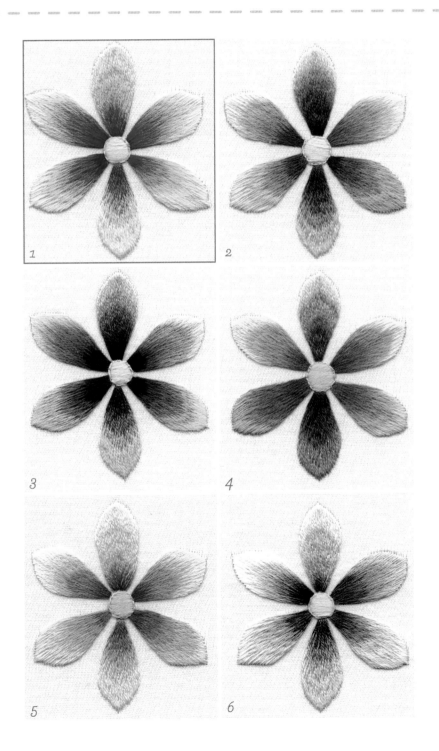

1. *Main colour*
   coral red

2. *Complementary opposite*
   avocado green

3. *Split complementary*
   blue-green

4. *Split complementary*
   olive green

5. *Triadic colour*
   gold

6. *Triadic colour*
   powder blue

REDS–TERRACOTTA

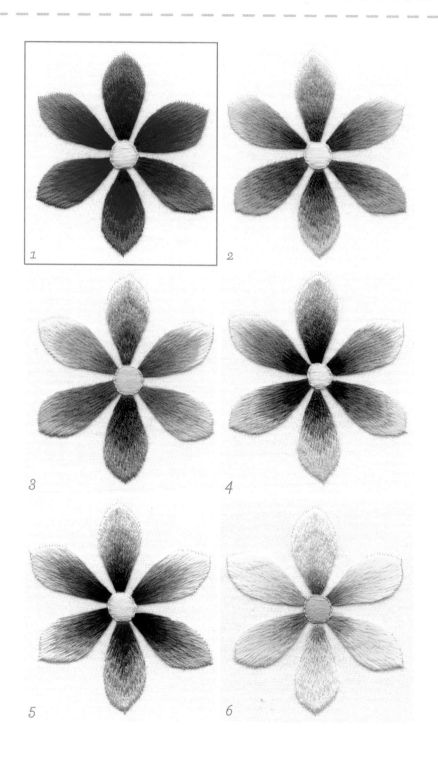

1. *Main colour*
   reds-terracotta

2. *Complementary*
   opposite
   green

3. *Split complementary*
   olive green

4. *Split complementary*
   blue-green

5. *Triadic colour*
   blue

6. *Triadic colour*
   yellow-saffron

84

OLD ROSE PINKS

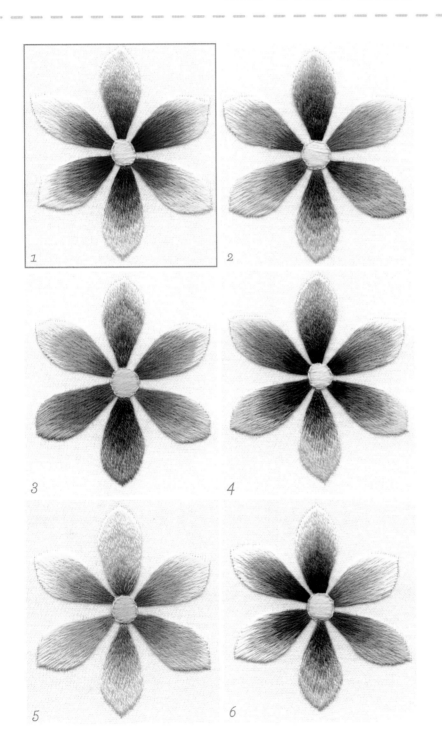

1. *Main colour*
   old rose pink

2. *Complementary*
   opposite
   avocado green

3. *Split complementary*
   olive green

4. *Split complementary*
   blue-green

5. *Triadic colour*
   gold

6. *Triadic colour*
   turquoise-teal

ROSE PINKS

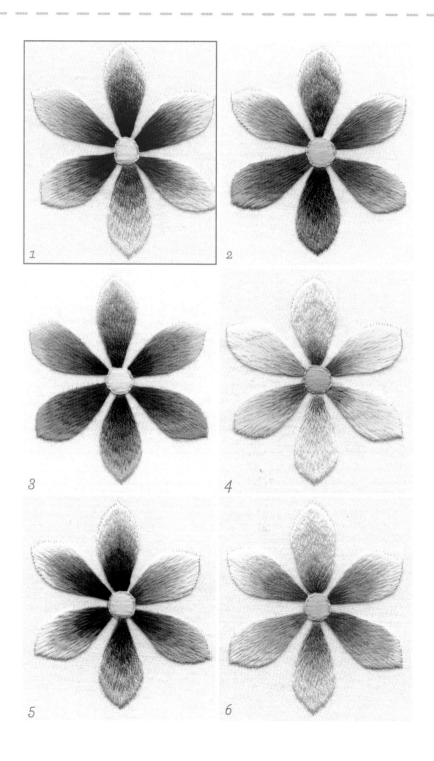

1. *Main colour*
   rose pink

2. *Complementary*
   opposite
   olive green

3. *Split complementary*
   green

4. *Split complementary*
   yellow-saffron

5. *Triadic colour*
   turquoise-teal

6. *Triadic colour*
   gold

PINKS–MAGENTA

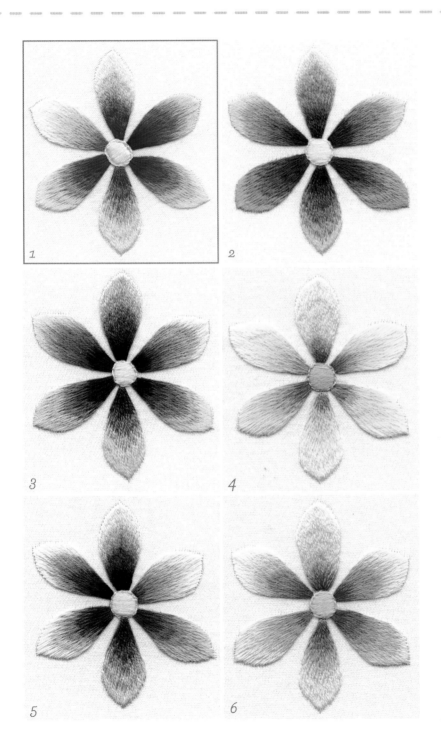

1. *Main colour*
   pinks-magenta

2. *Complementary*
   opposite
   green

3. *Split complementary*
   blue-green

4. *Split complementary*
   yellow-saffron

5. *Triadic colour*
   turquoise-teal

6. *Triadic colour*
   gold

MAUVE-GRAPE

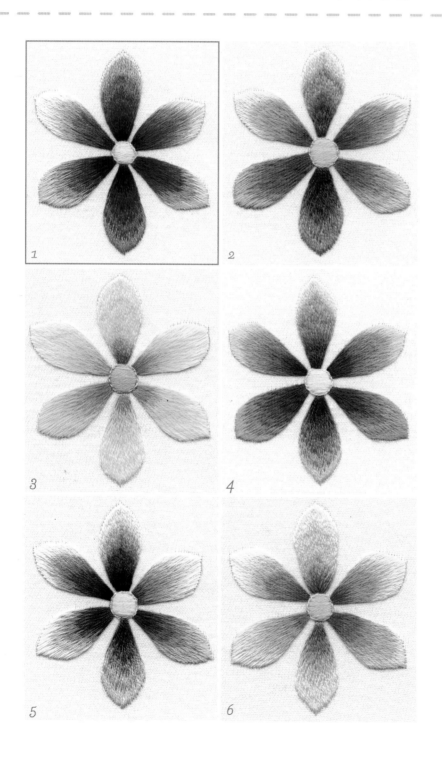

COMPLEMENTARY COLOURS

1. *Main colour*
   mauve-grape

2. *Complementary
   opposite*
   olive green

3. *Split complementary*
   yellow-orange

4. *Split complementary*
   green

5. *Triadic colour*
   turquoise-teal

6. *Triadic colour*
   gold

VIOLET–PURPLE

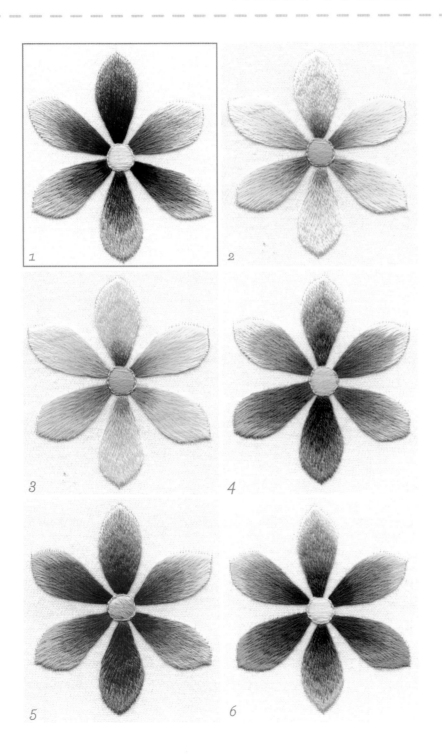

1. *Main colour*
   violet-purple

2. *Complementary*
   opposite
   yellow-saffron

3. *Split complementary*
   yellow-orange

4. *Split complementary*
   olive green

5. *Triadic colour*
   orange

6. *Triadic colour*
   green

POWDER BLUE

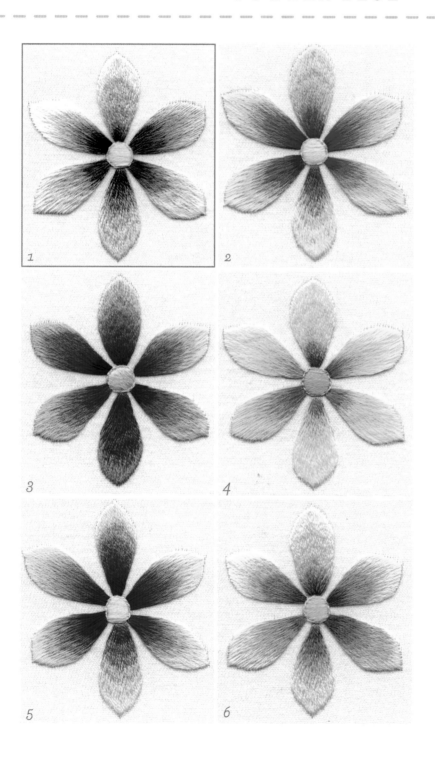

1. *Main colour*
   powder blue

2. *Complementary opposite*
   orange

3. *Split complementary*
   burnt orange

4. *Split complementary*
   yellow-orange

5. *Triadic colour*
   rose pink

6. *Triadic colour*
   gold/creams**

*is this gold?

90

BLUES

1. *Main colour*
   blue

2. *Complementary*
   opposite
   orange

3. *Split complementary*
   red-orange

4. *Split complementary*
   yellow-orange

5. *Triadic colour*
   yellow-saffron

6. *Triadic colour*
   coral red

TURQUOISE-TEAL

1. *Main colour*
   turquoise-teal

2. *Complementary opposite*
   golden brown

3. *Split complementary*
   reds-terracotta

4. *Split complementary*
   orange

5. *Triadic colour*
   pinks-magenta

6. *Triadic colour*
   gold

BLUE-GREENS

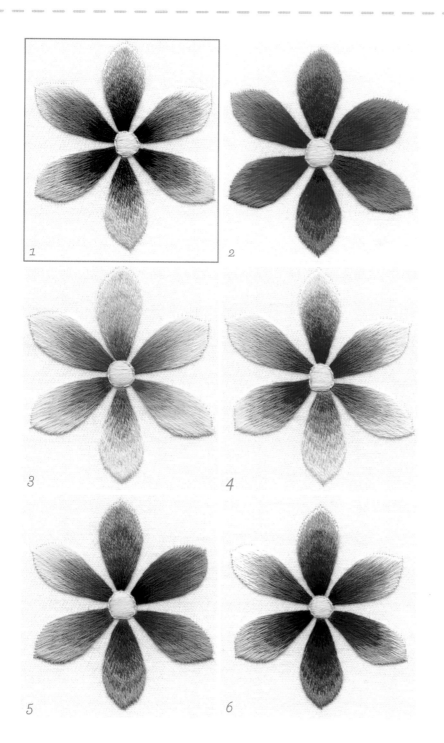

1. *Main colour*
   blue-green

2. *Complementary opposite*
   red-orange

3. *Split complementary*
   orange

4. *Split complementary*
   rose pink

5. *Triadic colour*
   golden brown

6. *Triadic colour*
   mauve-grape

GREENS

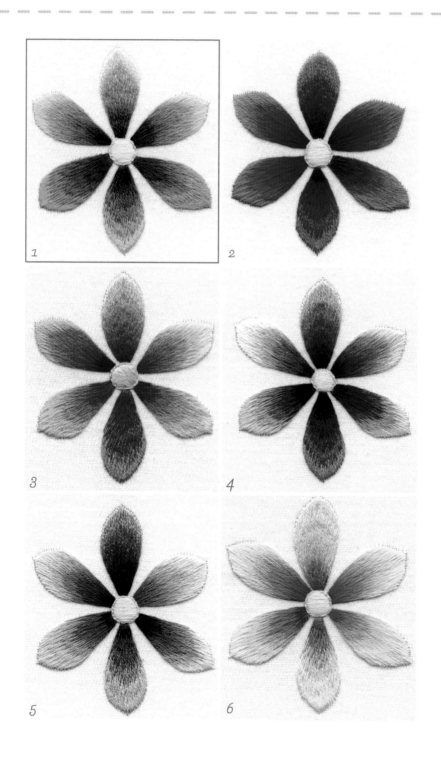

1. *Main colour*
   green

2. *Complementary*
   opposite
   reds-terracotta

3. *Split complementary*
   burnt orange

4. *Split complementary*
   mauve-grape

5. *Triadic colour*
   violet-purple

6. *Triadic colour*
   orange

94

AVOCADO GREEN

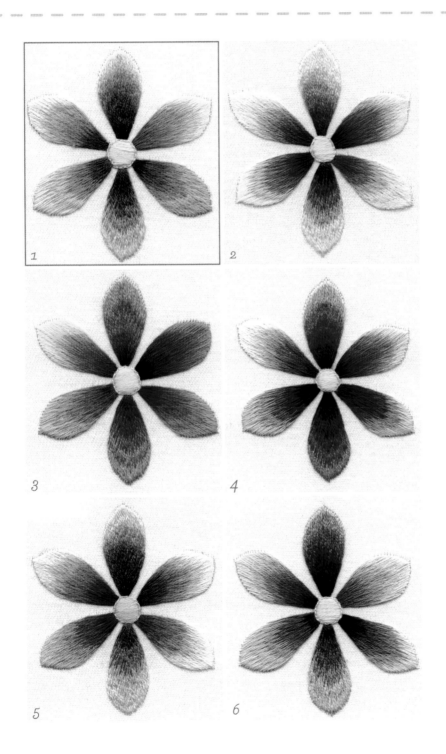

1. *Main colour*
   avocado green

2. *Complementary*
   opposite
   old rose

3. *Split complementary*
   golden brown

4. *Split complementary*
   mauve-grape

5. *Triadic colour*
   brown

6. *Triadic colour*
   violet-purple

OLIVE GREEN

1. *Main colour*
   olive green

2. *Complementary*
   opposite
   mauve-grape

3. *Split complementary*
   violet-purple

4. *Split complementary*
   red-terracotta

5. *Triadic colour*
   burnt orange

6. *Triadic colour*
   blue-violet

GOLD

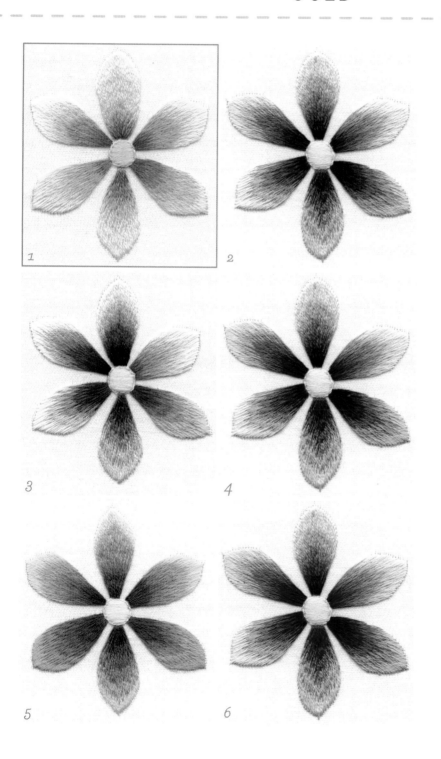

1. *Main colour*
   gold

2. *Complementary*
   opposite
   blue

3. *Split complementary*
   turquoise-teal

4. *Split complementary*
   blue-violet

5. *Triadic colour*
   green

6. *Triadic colour*
   plum

YELLOW–SAFFRON

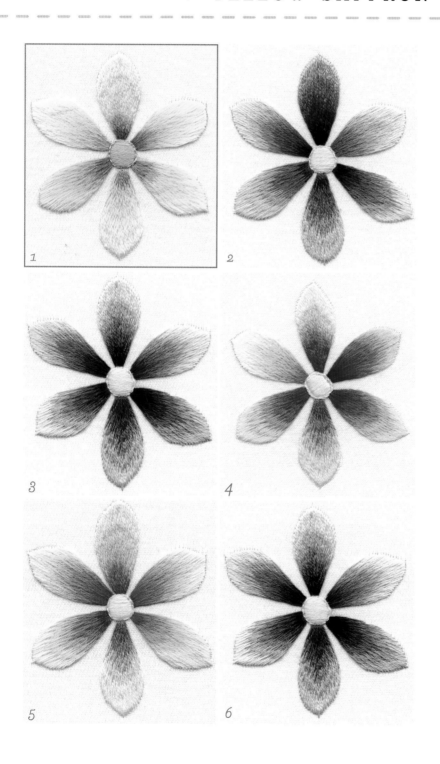

1. *Main colour*
   yellow-saffron

2. *Complementary*
   opposite
   violet-purple

3. *Split complementary*
   blue-violet

4. *Split complementary*
   pinks-magenta

5. *Triadic colour*
   coral red

6. *Triadic colour*
   blue

YELLOW-ORANGE

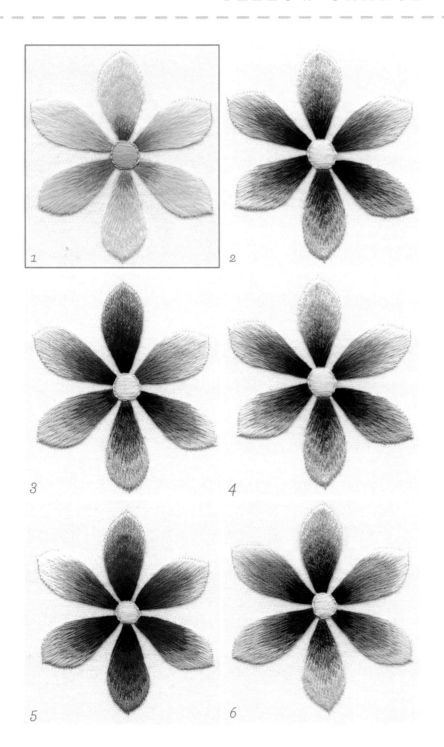

1. *Main colour*
   yellow-orange

2. *Complementary*
   opposite
   blue-violet

3. *Split complementary*
   violet-purple

4. *Split complementary*
   blue

5. *Triadic colour*
   mauve-grape

6. *Triadic colour*
   blue-green

ORANGE/BURNT ORANGE

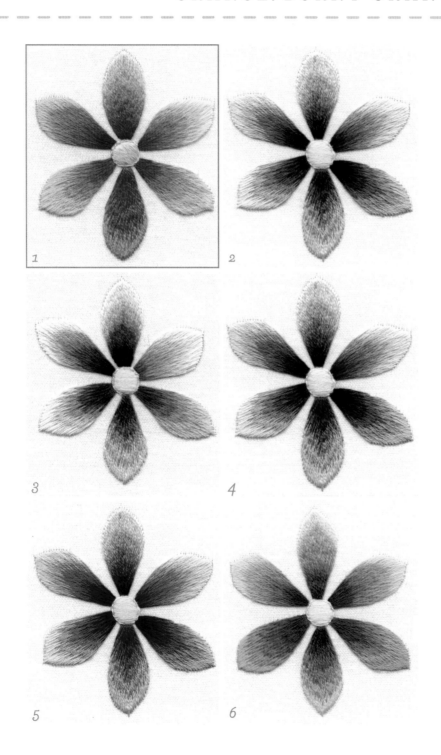

1. *Main colour*
   orange/burnt orange

2. *Complementary
   opposite*
   blue

3. *Split complementary*
   turquoise-teal

4. *Split complementary*
   blue-violet

5. *Triadic colour*
   purple

6. *Triadic colour*
   green

GOLDEN BROWN/COPPER

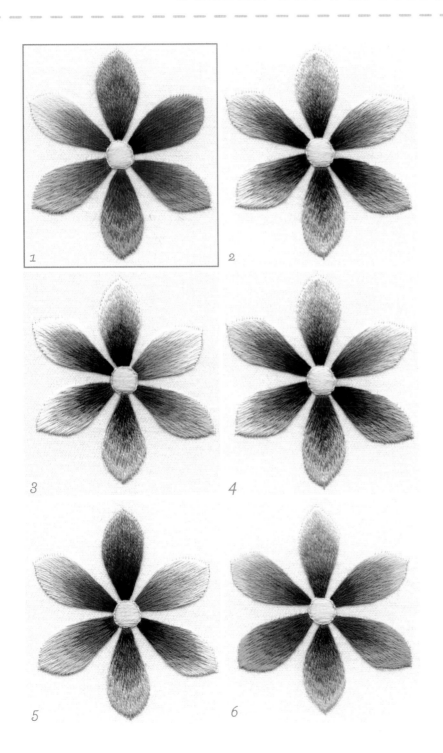

1. *Main colour*
golden brown/
copper

2. *Complementary*
   opposite
   blue

3. *Split complementary*
   turquoise-teal

4. *Split complementary*
   blue-violet

5. *Triadic colour*
   violet-purple

6. *Triadic colour*
   gr2een

BROWNS

COMPLEMENTARY COLOURS

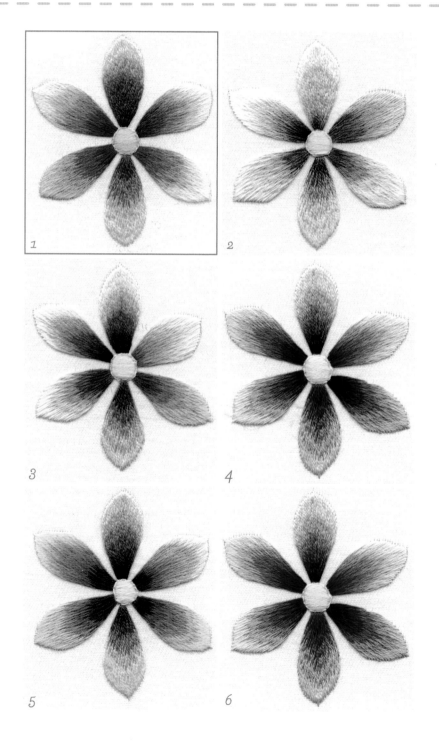

1. *Main colour*
   brown

2. *Complementary*
   opposite
   powder blue

3. *Split complementary*
   turquoise-teal

4. *Split complementary*
   blue-violet

5. *Triadic colour*
   blue-green

6. *Triadic colour*
   plum

GREY-BROWNS

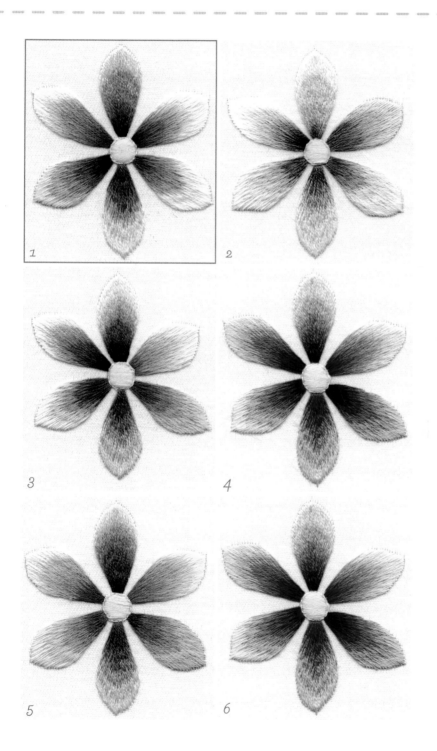

1. *Main colour*
   grey-brown

2. *Complementary opposite*
   powder blue

3. *Split complementary*
   turquoise-teal

4. *Split complementary*
   blue-violet

5. *Triadic colour*
   avocado green

6. *Triadic colour*
   plum

COLOUR SCHEMES

A picture of many colours proclaims images of many thoughts.

DONNA A. FAVORS

REMEMBER THAT when you choose colours for a needle painting project you will use the colours that you see in the picture you are reproducing. However, for decorative pieces such as stumpwork or crewel designs you will need to compose your own colour scheme.

Here are some combinations that may be helpful when choosing colour schemes for your decorative projects.

Each combination is made up of approximately three or four shades of colour, with tones of each. You can compose your own schemes by using a basic theme and including additional or similar shades and tones of these colours from the colour chart.

We often make the mistake of using too many colours in our embroidery, when it is better to use fewer colours and more shades or tones of those colours. A picture with too many colours is busy and distracting compared with a picture with fewer colours, which will be more soothing and visually pleasing.

On the page opposite is an example of a harmonious colour scheme using four main colours – burgundy, green, gold and white – with shades and tones of each.

Swatch colours

Since it is difficult to match up the exact print colour with the true thread colour I have provided DMC thread numbers for each colour swatch.

These are suggestions only and could be substituted with similar shades in brighter or duller tones according to your personal preference.

how to use a colour scheme

Chinese Bird & Flower Painting

BASED ON THIS SCHEME I have chosen the closest main colours from the scheme and built on these with shades and tones of each colour. As I have stitched I added or subtracted from these shades.

CORAL RED

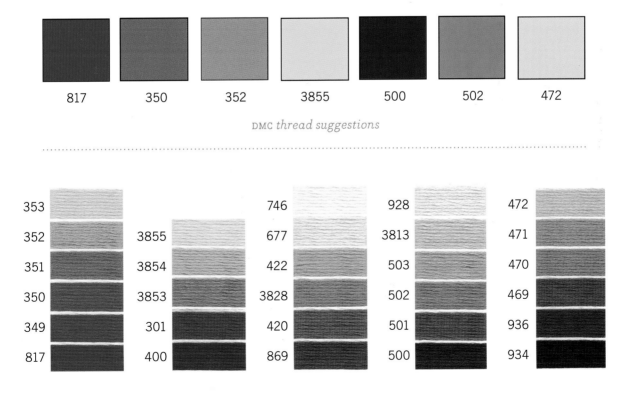

| 817 | 350 | 352 | 3855 | 500 | 502 | 472 |

DMC thread suggestions

353		746	928	472
352	3855	677	3813	471
351	3854	422	503	470
350	3853	3828	502	469
349	301	420	501	936
817	400	869	500	934

HARMONISING SCHEMES

This collection comprises harmonious combinations
for each colour group.

CORAL RED

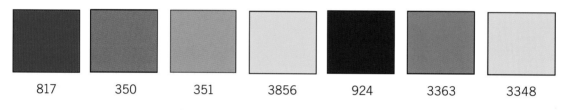

817   350   351   3856   924   3363   3348

DMC *thread suggestions*

RED

814   321   676   746   472   470   936

DMC *thread suggestions*

OLD ROSE PINKS

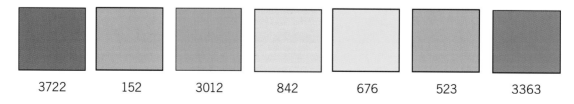

3722   152   3012   842   676   523   3363

DMC *thread suggestions*

ROSE PINKS

| 962 | 3326 | 3013 | 3790 | 407 | 739 | 3752 |

DMC *thread suggestions*

PINKS-MAGENTA

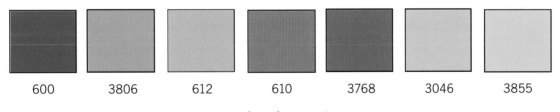

| 600 | 3806 | 612 | 610 | 3768 | 3046 | 3855 |

DMC *thread suggestions*

MAUVE-GRAPE

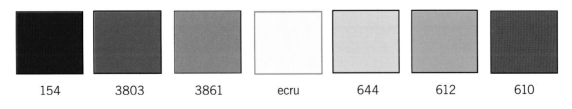

| 154 | 3803 | 3861 | ecru | 644 | 612 | 610 |

DMC *thread suggestions*

HARMONISING SCHEMES

PLUM

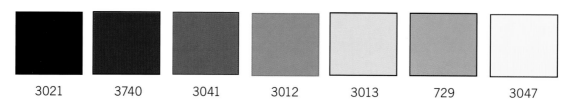

| 3021 | 3740 | 3041 | 3012 | 3013 | 729 | 3047 |

DMC *thread suggestions*

SHADES OF BURGUNDY

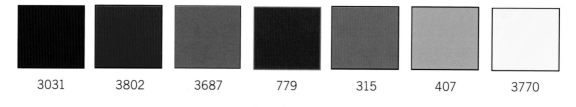

| 3031 | 3802 | 3687 | 779 | 315 | 407 | 3770 |

DMC *thread suggestions*

VIOLET-PURPLE

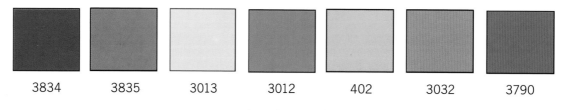

| 3834 | 3835 | 3013 | 3012 | 402 | 3032 | 3790 |

DMC *thread suggestions*

BLUE-VIOLET

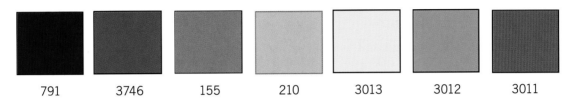

| 791 | 3746 | 155 | 210 | 3013 | 3012 | 3011 |

DMC *thread suggestions*

POWDER BLUE

| 809 | 800 | 340 | 353 | 524 | 522 | 520 |

DMC *thread suggestions*

BLUE

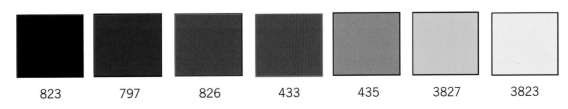

| 823 | 797 | 826 | 433 | 435 | 3827 | 3823 |

DMC *thread suggestions*

HARMONISING SCHEMES

SHADES OF BLUE

| 939 | 930 | 932 | 3753 | 3842 | 518 | 3761 |

DMC *thread suggestions*

TURQUOISE-TEAL

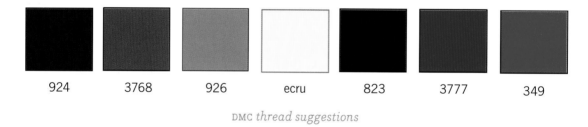

| 924 | 3768 | 926 | ecru | 823 | 3777 | 349 |

DMC *thread suggestions*

SHADES OF TEAL

| 924 | 3768 | 926 | 738 | 3813 | 3849 | 3847 |

DMC *thread suggestions*

COLOUR SCHEMES

BLUE-GREENS

| 561 | 562 | 966 | 353 | 666 | 3705 | 3706 |

DMC *thread suggestions*

AVOCADO GREEN

| 935 | 937 | 471 | 472 | 422 | 3831 | 3833 |

DMC *thread suggestions*

OLIVE GREENS

| 730 | 732 | 734 | 3047 | 350 | 352 | 353 |

DMC *thread suggestions*

HARMONISING SCHEMES

SHADES OF GREEN

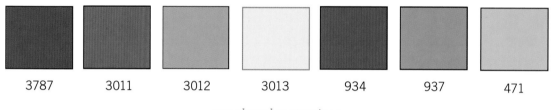

| 3787 | 3011 | 3012 | 3013 | 934 | 937 | 471 |

DMC *thread suggestions*

GOLD

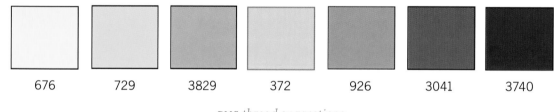

| 676 | 729 | 3829 | 372 | 926 | 3041 | 3740 |

DMC *thread suggestions*

YELLOW-SAFFRON

| 732 | 734 | 3821 | 727 | 3078 | 791 | 3746 |

DMC *thread suggestions*

YELLOW-ORANGE

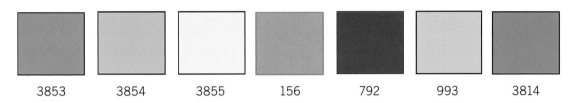

| 3853 | 3854 | 3855 | 156 | 792 | 993 | 3814 |

DMC *thread suggestions*

ORANGE/BURNT ORANGE

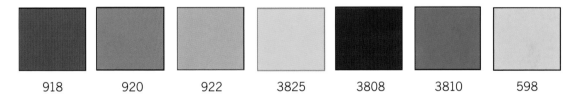

| 918 | 920 | 922 | 3825 | 3808 | 3810 | 598 |

DMC *thread suggestions*

APRICOT

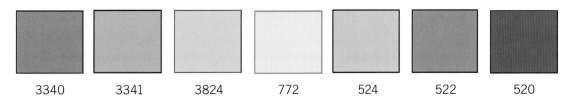

| 3340 | 3341 | 3824 | 772 | 524 | 522 | 520 |

DMC *thread suggestions*

HARMONISING SCHEMES

RED-ORANGE

| 3857 | 355 | 350 | 3047 | 950 | 3051 | 3012 |

DMC *thread suggestions*

GOLDEN BROWN/COPPER

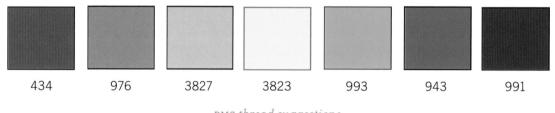

| 434 | 976 | 3827 | 3823 | 993 | 943 | 991 |

DMC *thread suggestions*

BROWNS

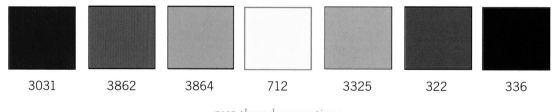

| 3031 | 3862 | 3864 | 712 | 3325 | 322 | 336 |

DMC *thread suggestions*

GREY-BROWNS

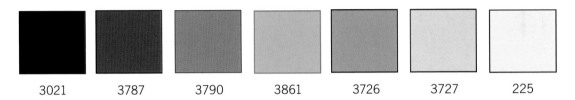

| 3021 | 3787 | 3790 | 3861 | 3726 | 3727 | 225 |

DMC *thread suggestions*

NATURAL

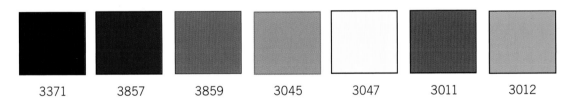

| 3371 | 3857 | 3859 | 3045 | 3047 | 3011 | 3012 |

DMC *thread suggestions*

DESIGN SCHEMES

*This collection consists of original schemes,
designed around a theme.*

A GOOD YEAR

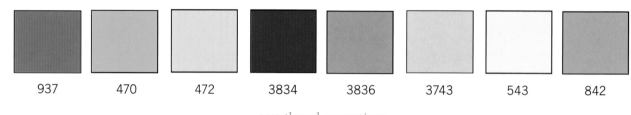

937 470 472 3834 3836 3743 543 842

DMC *thread suggestions*

ANNE OF GREEN GABLES

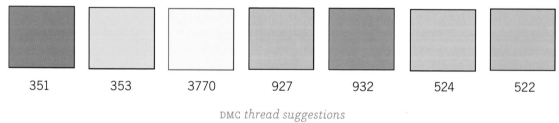

351 353 3770 927 932 524 522

DMC *thread suggestions*

AS GOOD AS IT GETS

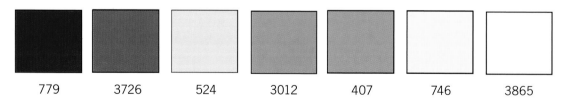

779 3726 524 3012 407 746 3865

DMC *thread suggestions*

They are named after my favourite movies, although it may take some imagination to see the connection – I had fun compiling them and hope it inspires you to look outside the box for some different schemes!

AUSTRALIA

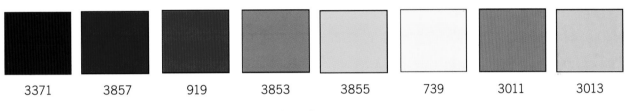

| 3371 | 3857 | 919 | 3853 | 3855 | 739 | 3011 | 3013 |

DMC *thread suggestions*

AUTUMN IN NEW YORK

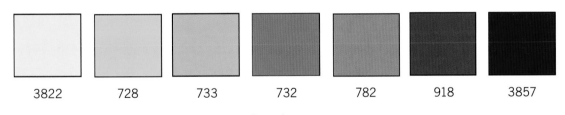

| 3822 | 728 | 733 | 732 | 782 | 918 | 3857 |

DMC *thread suggestions*

CHOCOLAT

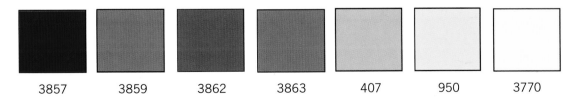

| 3857 | 3859 | 3862 | 3863 | 407 | 950 | 3770 |

DMC *thread suggestions*

DESIGN SCHEMES

THE DEVIL WEARS PRADA

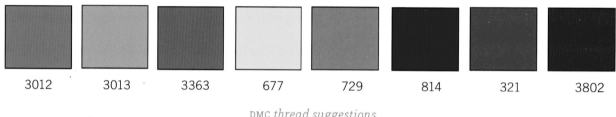

| 3012 | 3013 | 3363 | 677 | 729 | 814 | 321 | 3802 |

DMC *thread suggestions*

ELIZABETH

| 3726 | 3727 | 3041 | 3835 | 161 | 436 | 520 | 524 |

DMC *thread suggestions*

EMMA

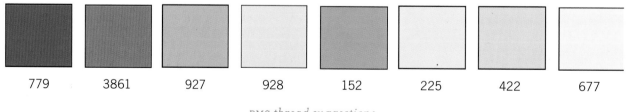

| 779 | 3861 | 927 | 928 | 152 | 225 | 422 | 677 |

DMC *thread suggestions*

FATHER OF THE BRIDE

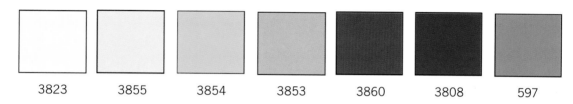

| 3823 | 3855 | 3854 | 3853 | 3860 | 3808 | 597 |

DMC *thread suggestions*

FOUR WEDDINGS AND A FUNERAL

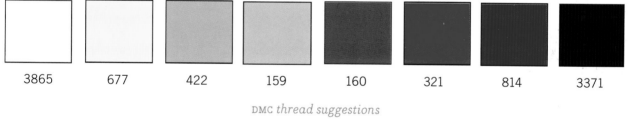

| 3865 | 677 | 422 | 159 | 160 | 321 | 814 | 3371 |

DMC *thread suggestions*

FRENCH KISS

| 809 | 798 | 336 | 3856 | 977 | 758 | 407 |

DMC *thread suggestions*

DESIGN SCHEMES

THE GREAT GATSBY

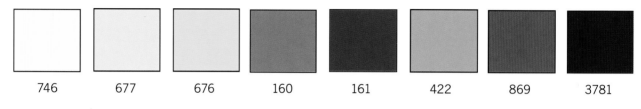

| 746 | 677 | 676 | 160 | 161 | 422 | 869 | 3781 |

DMC *thread suggestions*

LADIES IN LAVENDER

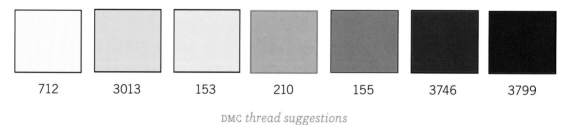

| 712 | 3013 | 153 | 210 | 155 | 3746 | 3799 |

DMC *thread suggestions*

LITTLE WOMEN

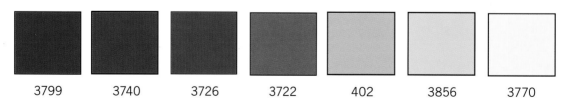

| 3799 | 3740 | 3726 | 3722 | 402 | 3856 | 3770 |

DMC *thread suggestions*

MY BEST FRIEND'S WEDDING

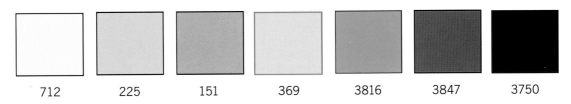

712   225   151   369   3816   3847   3750

DMC *thread suggestions*

OUT OF AFRICA

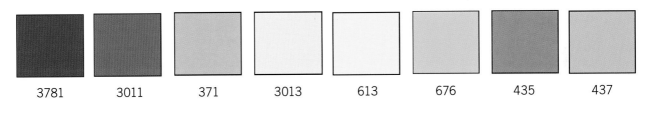

3781   3011   371   3013   613   676   435   437

DMC *thread suggestions*

OUT TO SEA

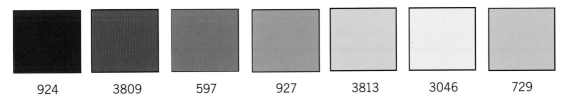

924   3809   597   927   3813   3046   729

DMC *thread suggestions*

DESIGN SCHEMES

A PASSAGE TO INDIA

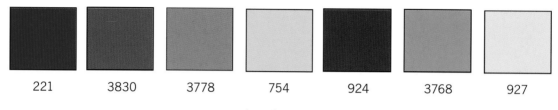

| 221 | 3830 | 3778 | 754 | 924 | 3768 | 927 |

DMC *thread suggestions*

PERSUASION

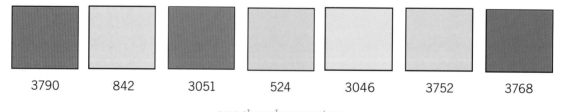

| 3790 | 842 | 3051 | 524 | 3046 | 3752 | 3768 |

DMC *thread suggestions*

PRETTY WOMAN

| 3743 | 3042 | 3041 | 3740 | 524 | 503 | 3768 |

DMC *thread suggestions*

PRIDE AND PREJUDICE

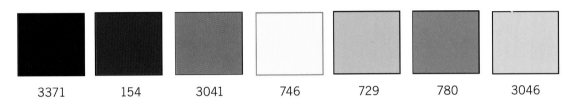

3371 | 154 | 3041 | 746 | 729 | 780 | 3046

DMC thread suggestions

SENSE AND SENSIBILITY

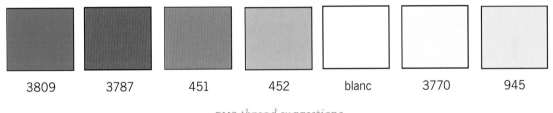

3809 | 3787 | 451 | 452 | blanc | 3770 | 945

DMC thread suggestions

THE SOUND OF MUSIC

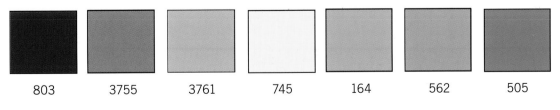

803 | 3755 | 3761 | 745 | 164 | 562 | 505

DMC thread suggestions

DESIGN SCHEMES

TEA WITH MUSSOLINI

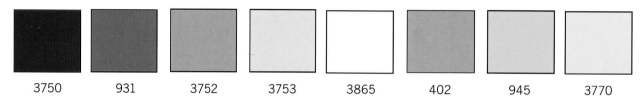

3750 931 3752 3753 3865 402 945 3770

DMC *thread suggestions*

THE HOLIDAY

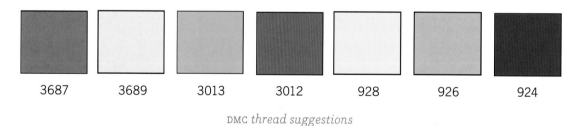

3687 3689 3013 3012 928 926 924

DMC *thread suggestions*

THE WEDDING PLANNER

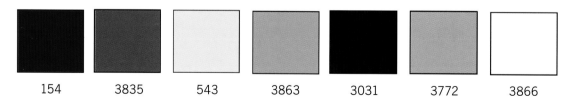

154 3835 543 3863 3031 3772 3866

DMC *thread suggestions*

COLOUR SCHEMES

TITANIC

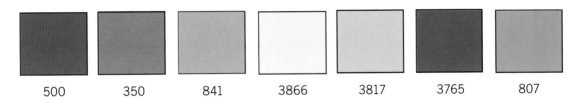

| 500 | 350 | 841 | 3866 | 3817 | 3765 | 807 |

DMC *thread suggestions*

THE TUDORS

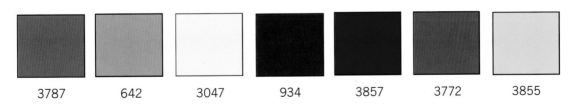

| 3787 | 642 | 3047 | 934 | 3857 | 3772 | 3855 |

DMC *thread suggestions*

DESIGN SCHEMES

UNDER THE TUSCAN SUN

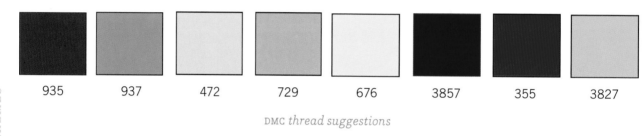

| 935 | 937 | 472 | 729 | 676 | 3857 | 355 | 3827 |

DMC *thread suggestions*

YOUNG VICTORIA

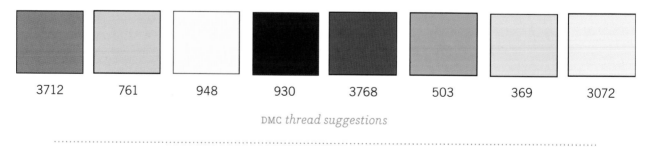

| 3712 | 761 | 948 | 930 | 3768 | 503 | 369 | 3072 |

DMC *thread suggestions*

the
PROJECTS

French Rose

Adapted from Rosa Gallica Maheka, *French Rose 'Violacea', by Pierre-Joseph Redouté.*

I chose this rose to represent red because of the deep, vibrant shades of this colour so evident in the petals.

MATERIALS

vanilla or off-white linen/ cotton satin, approx. 30 x 32 cm (12 x 12½ in)

fine batiste for backing, approx. 30 x 32 cm (12 x 12½ in) (optional)

DMC stranded cotton, and silks, as listed in key

crewel needles sizes 9, 10

frame approx. 27 x 30 cm (10½ x 12 in) or hoop 25 cm (10 in) diameter

tracing outline
actual size: reduce or enlarge as desired

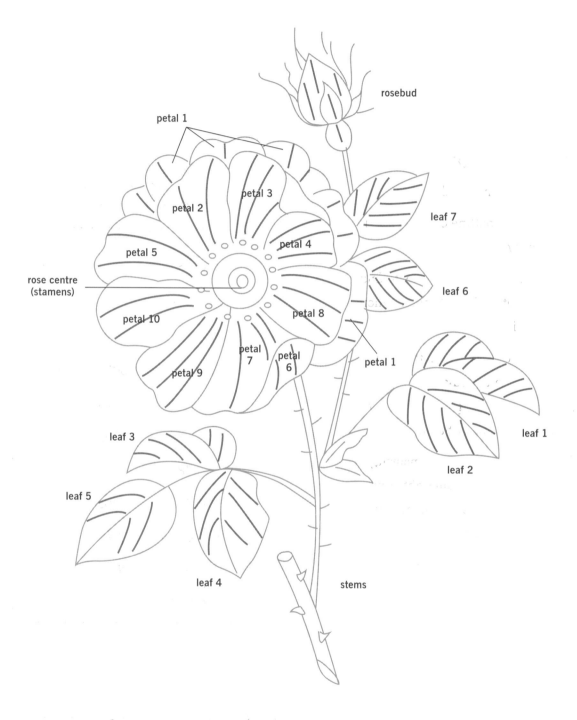

rosebud

petal 1

petal 2

petal 3

petal 4

petal 5

leaf 7

rose centre
(stamens)

petal 8

leaf 6

petal 10

petal
7

petal
6

petal 1

petal 9

leaf 1

leaf 2

leaf 3

leaf 5

leaf 4

stems

stitch guide

PREPARATION

Wash and iron the fabric.

Transfer the outline onto the centre of the linen fabric.

Pull a thread at right angles to find the straight grain on both the linen and backing fabric.

Line up the fabrics with the grain and overcast the edges of both pieces of fabric together on a sewing machine or tack by hand.

Mount in hoop or frame ensuring that the fabric is drum tight. You may need to adjust this occasionally as you stitch to keep it taut.

thread key

DMC stranded cotton and Eterna silk are used in this project.

DMC		Eterna
304	935	940
321	936	1110
371	3011	3970
372	3012	4470
729	3013	
780	3051	
782	3348	
814	3801	
815	3821	
902	3822	
934		

One strand of thread is used throughout this project unless otherwise indicated.

METHOD

stems key	
A 3013	E 372
B 3348	F 371
C 3012	G Eterna 4470
D 3011	H Eterna 940

1: Stems

Fill each stem with adjacent rows of split stitch, shading from left to right across the stem in A, B, C and D. On the narrow stems use E, F and C.

Work a line of split stitch in G on the right side to create a shadow.

Work the thorns along the stem with straight stitches in H. The large thorns will need two straight stitches into a point and the smaller one straight stitch.

Fill the leaf stems with split stitch in A and C. Fill the small leaves with satin stitch in A and C.

rosebud key	
A 3012	E 304
B 936	F 814
C 934	G 902
D Eterna 3970	H Eterna 1110

2: Rosebud

Outline and pad the bud with straight stitches across in E. Fill the bud with long and short stitch from the outside edge in towards the centre using shades E, F and G and add a few straight stitches for shadows in H.

Fill the base of the bud with padded satin stitch in B. Blend in a few straight stitches in C at the base.

Fill the large sepal with long and short stitch using shades A, B and C

Fill the smaller sepals with split stitch in shades A, B and C.

Take one strand fine silk and work details in straight stitches to create shadows in D.

3: Leaves

Outline each leaf in split stitch before filling with long and short stitch on either side of the centre vein.

Work from the outside edge in towards the centre vein, staying in line with the guidelines.

leaves key	
A 371	F Eterna 940
B 3012	G 3013
C 3011	H 935
D 3051	I 934
E Eterna 4470	

Leaf 1
top = B, C, D
bottom = G, B, D
Leaf 2
top = G, B, C, D
bottom = I, H, C, B
Leaf 3
top = C, D, H
bottom = A, B, C
Leaf 4
left = C, H, I
right = B, C, D, H
Leaf 5
top = A, B, C
bottom = H, C, B

leaf 1 (top) and 2

leaf 3

leaf 4

leaf 5

Leaf 6

Leaf 7

Leaf 6
top = A, B, D
bottom = A, B, C, D
Leaf 7
top = A, B, C, D
bottom = A, B, C, D

Work the centre veins in split stitch with one strand E. Add tiny little straight stitches at the edge of the leaf, to create an irregular appearance, in F.

rose petals key	
A 3801	D 815
B 321	E 902
C 304	F Eterna 1110

4: Rose petals

Outline each petal individually with split stitch, using one strand C, before stitching the next.

Fill each petal with long and short stitch in order: petals 1, 2, 3, 4, 5, 6, 7, 8, 9 and 10 using:

Petal 1 (four petals)
C, D, E, F (these are the back petals)
Petal 2
A, B, C, D, E, F
Petal 3
A, B, C, D, E; add some F under the turnover
Petal 4
A, B, C, D, E; add some F under the turnover; pad the turnover with satin stitch and fill with B, C, E

Petal 5

A, B, C, D, E

Petal 6

D, E, F; pad the turnover with satin stitch
and fill with B, C, E

Petal 7

A, B, C, D, E

Petal 8

B, C, D, E, F; pad the turnover with satin
stitch and fill with B, C, E

Petal 9

A, B, C, D, E, F

Petal 10

A, B, C, D, E, F

Take one strand F and work a line of split
stitch under the overlap of each petal to
create definition.

Deepen shadows where necessary by
blending in additional stitches in F.

5: Rose centre

Stitch the inner ring with padded satin
stitch in A as shown in the picture. Fill
inside with a few French knots in B and C.

Make straight stitches from the inner ring
out towards the outer ring in A, C and E.

Work French knots, using one strand and
two twists, around the edge of the outer
ring in A, B, C, D and E.

rose centre key	
A 3822	D 782
B 3821	E 780
C 729	

Camellia Japonica

Adapted from Camellia japonica Linnaeus *'Alba Simplex', by Pierre-Joseph Redouté.*

The sugary pink of this flower's petals made it a natural choice for representing the colour pink.

MATERIALS

vanilla or off-white linen/ cotton satin, approx. 30 x 32 cm (12 x 12½ in)

fine batiste for backing, approx. 30 x 32 cm (12 x 12½ in) (optional)

DMC stranded cotton, and silks, as listed in key

crewel needles sizes 9, 10

frame approx. 27 x 30 cm (10½ x 12 in) or hoop 25 cm (10 in) diameter

tracing outline
actual size: reduce or enlarge as desired

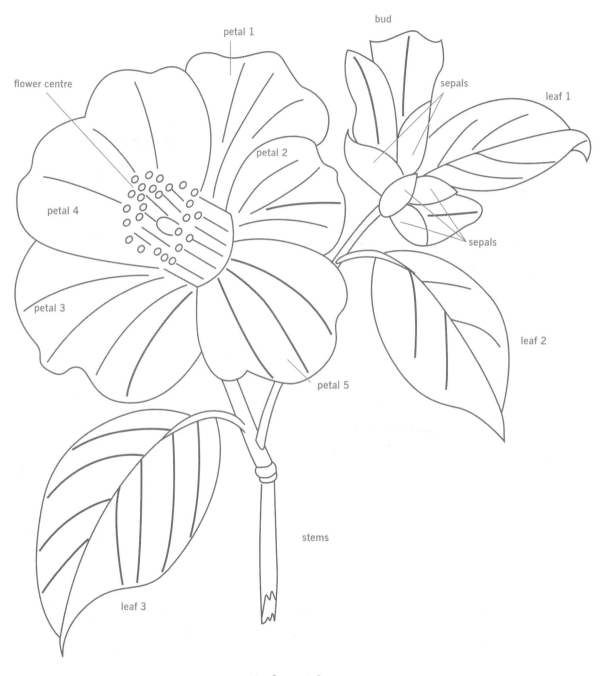

petal 1

bud

flower centre

sepals

leaf 1

petal 2

petal 4

petal 3

sepals

leaf 2

petal 5

stems

leaf 3

stitch guide

PREPARATION

Wash and iron the fabric.

Transfer the outline onto the centre of the linen fabric.

Pull a thread at right angles to find the straight grain on both the linen and backing fabric.

Line up the fabrics with the grain and overcast the edges of both pieces of fabric together on a sewing machine or tack by hand.

Mount in hoop or frame ensuring that the fabric is drum tight. You may need to adjust this occasionally as you stitch to keep it taut.

One strand of thread is used throughout this project unless otherwise indicated.

thread key

DMC stranded cotton and Eterna silk are used in this project.

DMC		
151	819	3364
319	834	3688
371	934	3731
471	937	3733
524	3021	3781
603	3032	blanc
604	3033	3833
605	3328	3822
610	3345	3823
640	3346	3854
772	3347	3855
818	3348	3865
Eterna		
4620		

METHOD

stems key

A	3033	F	3021
B	524	G	3364
C	3032	H	3348
D	640	I	471
E	3781	J	937

1: Stems

Fill the stems with adjacent rows of split stitch shading with A, B, C, D, E and F.

Work across the stems from left to right, light to dark.

You will need to decrease the number of shades as the stems narrow – that is, use A, C, D and E.

Add a few straight stitches in G at the base of the stem.

Leaf stems – work in split stitch using H, I and J.

leaves key	
A 772	E 3346
B 3348	F 3345
C 471	G 319
D 3347	H 934

2: Leaves

Outline each leaf with split stitch (leave the centre vein free) before filling each side with long and short stitch from the outside in towards the centre vein.

Use shades for each side as follows:

leaf 1

Leaf 1
bottom = D, E, F, G
top = D, E, F, G, H
Leaf 2
left side = C, D, E, F, G, H
right side = D, E, F, G
Leaf 3
left side = A, B, C, D, E, F
right side = D, E, F, G, H

leaf 2

Fill the centre vein of each leaf with split stitch in C.

leaf 3

buds key	
petals	sepals
A 819	A 772
B 818	B 3348
C 151	C 471
D 605	D 3347
E 604	E 3346

flower petals key	
A 3733	G blanc
B 3688	H 3833
C 604	I 3328
D 605	J 3731
E 151	K 603
F 819	

petal 1

petal 2

3: Buds

Outline each bud petal with split stitch. Fill the petals with long and short stitch using A, B, C, D and E.

Fill the sepals with long and short stitch using A, B, C, D and E.

4: Flower petals

Outline each petal with split stitch before filling with long and short stitch from the outside edge in towards the centre.

The placement of shades varies for each petal depending on where the light falls. Use following shades:

Petal 1
A + B (in first row), C, D, E, F
Petal 2
A, B, C, D, E, F
Petal 3
E, F, G, F, E, D, C, H, I
Petal 4
E, F, E, D, C, H, I
Petal 5
J, K, C, D, E, F

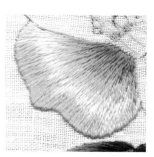

petal 3

petal 4

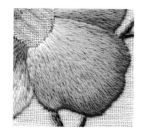

petal 5

5: Flower centre

Work the background area of the centre first in long and short stitch, using A, B and C.

Next work the central stamens in straight stitches using D, E and G, and add some small stitches at the base in C.

Finally, work random French knots using two twists in C, G and H.

Enhance the shadows and details with one strand Eterna silk in I.

flower centre key	
A 3855	F 834
B 3854	G 371
C 610	H 3822
D 3865	I Eterna 4620
E 3823	

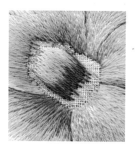

Iris 'Spartan'

An adaptation of the painting Iris 'Spartan' *by Graham Rust (1995)**

I chose this iris to represent the colour mauve, due to the interesting shades of wine and mauve that appear in the petals.

MATERIALS

vanilla or off-white linen/ cotton satin, approx. 32 x 35 cm (12½ x 14 in)

fine batiste for backing, approx. 32 x 35 cm (12½ x 14 in) (optional)

DMC stranded cotton, and silks, as listed in key

crewel needles sizes 9, 10

frame approx. 27 x 30 cm (10½ x 12 in) or hoop 25 cm (10 in) diameter

* Permission granted by Shirley Sherwood, author of Contemporary Botanical Artists

tracing outline
actual size: reduce or enlarge as desired

T Burr 09

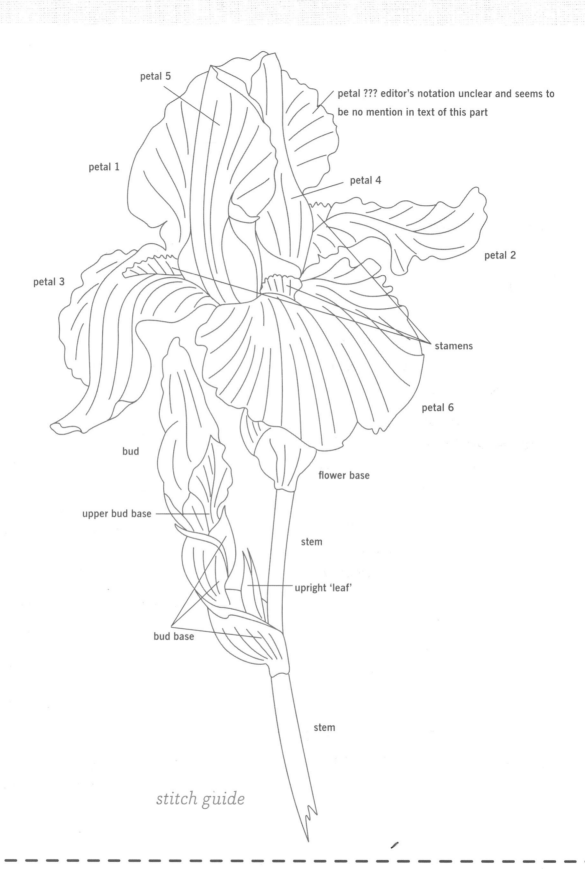

petal 5

petal ??? editor's notation unclear and seems to be no mention in text of this part

petal 1

petal 4

petal 2

petal 3

stamens

petal 6

bud

flower base

upper bud base

stem

upright 'leaf'

bud base

stem

stitch guide

MAUVE PROJECT: *Iris Spartan*

PREPARATION

Wash and iron the fabric.

Transfer the outline onto the centre of the linen fabric.

Pull a thread at right angles to find the straight grain on both the linen and backing fabric.

Line up the fabrics with the grain and overcast the edges of both pieces of fabric together on a sewing machine or tack by hand.

Mount in hoop or frame ensuring that the fabric is drum tight. You may need to adjust this occasionally as you stitch to keep it taut.

One strand of thread is used throughout this project unless otherwise indicated.

thread key

DMC stranded cotton is used in this project.

DMC		
152	945	3722
154	975	3740
221	3011	3743
223	3012	3778
315	3013	3787
336	3021	3857
372	3042	3866
402	3041	3799
453	3046	3821
471	3047	3822
472	3328	3829
610	3348	3834
746	3712	
833	3721	

METHOD

stem key

A 746	E 3348
B 3047	F 471
C 3046	G 3012
D 472	H 3011

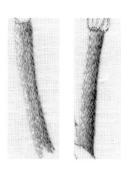

bud base key

A 3866	F 3013
B 746	G 3348
C 3047	H 3012
D 3822	I 610
E 372	J 3021

1: Stem

Start with the lower half of the stem. Fill with adjacent rows of split stitch from left to right, light to dark, in A, B, C, D, E, F and G.

Work the upper half in the same way, using B, D, E, F, G and H.

2: Bud base

Start with the top back areas as shown. Outline each section with split stitch before filling in F. Fill with long and short stitch using D, C, F and H.

Fill the front left section with long and short, using D, C, B and A.

Fill the front right section with long and short, using B, C, E, F, G and H.

Fill the small upright 'leaf' next to the upper part of the stem with long and short, using C, E, F and H.

Fill the bottom section as before, using A, B, C, E, F, H.

Add shadows under the turnovers of each section in split stitch using I and J.

Finally, fill the turnovers with adjacent rows of split stitch in A. Slightly cover the shadow lines but leave a little of the shadows peeping out as shown.

Fill the upper section of the bud base as before with long and short stitch, using C, D, E, F and H. Work shadows with I and J.

3: Bud

Next work the bud. Start at the tip of the bud outline with split stitch in D and fill with long and short stitch using G, F, E, D, C, B and A.

The first row will be a mix (alternating stitches) of G and F. The second row will be a mix of F and E. Thereafter, work shading in the normal way.

This is a good example of mixing shades to achieve a colour that cannot be found on the DMC chart. The iris colour is a dirty blue/plum – by mixing the blue, grey and plum we can achieve a colour close to the one we need.

	bud key	
A 453		E 3740
B 3743		F 336
C 3042		G 3799
D 3041		

flower base key	
A 3047	D 610
B 3822	E 3787
C 833	F 3799

4: Flower base

Refer to picture of finished project.

Outline with split stitch in B and fill the flower base with long and short stitch using A, B, C, D and E. Add shadows afterwards with F.

petal 1 key	
A 3712	C 3721
B 3328	D 221

petal 1

5: Iris petals

Petal 1 Start with the back left petal; note it has two sections, one either side of the central standards (check stitch diagram). Only the left side appears in this detail photo. Outline with split stitch in D. Fill both sections of the petal with long and short stitch from the outside in towards the centre, using D, C, B, A.

152

Petal 2 Outline this horizontal petal on the right with split stitch in B. Work the petal in two sections, starting with the lower, front section. Fill with long and short stitch, working from the outside in towards the base. Use A, B, D, E, F and G, and finally blend in C.

On the second half (upper back), fill with long and short stitch, using B, D, E, F and G.

Petal 3 Start at the tip of this horizontal petal on the left and work up towards the centre. Outline the petal with split stitch in C.

Fill the front section of the petal with long and short stitch, shading with C, D, E and F. Work G and H on the small turnovers. Reverse shades to F, E, D and C then begin to blend in shades of B and A.

On the second half of the petal (back section), blend with H, G, F, E, D and C.

petal 2 key			
A	152	E	315
B	223	F	3740
C	3712	G	154
D	3722		

petal 2

petal 3 key			
A	402	E	315
B	3778	F	3740
C	223	G	3834
D	3722	H	154

petal 3

petal 4 key	
A 223	E 221
B 3722	F 3834
C 3721	G 154
D 315	

petal 4

Petal 4 This petal is partly hidden by the other standard petal. Start at the top and work down. Outline the petal in split stitch in B. Fill with long and short stitch in A, B, C, D, E, F and G. Add shadows in F and G as shown.

Petal 5 Work from the tip down. Outline the petal with split stitch in B.

Fill with long and short stitch in A, B, C, D, E, F, G and H,

Continue until you reach the base.

Work the piece at the base, separately using D, I and J.

petal 5 key	
A 152	F 3834
B 223	G 154
C 3722	H 221
D 3721	I 3857
E 315	

petal 5, work from the tip down

petal 5, base

154

Petal 6 Outline this petal, the large fall at the front of the flower, with split stitch using D.

Start on the right hand side of petal at the base and work up towards the centre as shown in the first photograph. Fill with long and short stitch using A, B, C, D, E, F and G.

Fill the left hand side of the petal with long and short stitch using A, B, C, D, E, F and G.

Towards the top of the petal start blending in H, I, J and K as highlights.

Go back and add shadows in split stitch with F and G to enhance all dark areas of the flower petals.

6: Stamens

Fill the three patches of stamens with short straight stitches, using C, B and A. Angle the stitches to produce a feathery look

petal 6 key	
A 3722	G 3857
B 3721	H 152
C 315	I 223
D 3740	J 945
E 3834	K 402
F 154	

petal 6

stamens key		
A 3821	B 3829	C 975

Crocus sativus

Adapted from Crocus sativus Linnaeus *(Iridaceae), by Pierre-Joseph Redouté.*

This flower was an obvious choice for its glorious purple petals.

MATERIALS

vanilla or off-white linen/ cotton satin, approx. 30 x 32 cm (12 x 12½ in)

fine batiste for backing, approx. 30 x 32 cm (12 x 12½ in) (optional)

DMC stranded cotton, and silks, as listed in key

crewel needles sizes 9, 10

frame approx. 27 x 30 cm (10½ x 12 in) or hoop 25 cm (10 in) diameter

tracing outline
actual size: reduce or enlarge as desired

TBurr 10

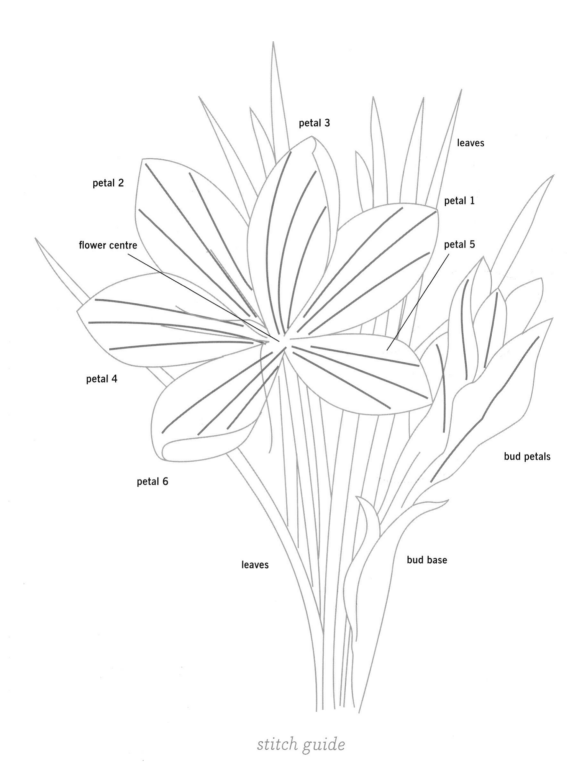

petal 3

leaves

petal 2

petal 1

flower centre

petal 5

petal 4

bud petals

petal 6

leaves

bud base

stitch guide

PREPARATION

Wash and iron the fabric.

Transfer the outline onto the centre of the linen fabric.

Pull a thread at right angles to find the straight grain on both the linen and backing fabric.

Line up the fabrics with the grain and overcast the edges of both pieces of fabric together on a sewing machine or tack by hand.

Mount in hoop or frame ensuring that the fabric is drum tight. You may need to adjust this occasionally as you stitch to keep it taut.

One strand of thread is used throughout this project unless otherwise indicated.

thread key

DMC and two Anchor stranded cottons are used in this project. I have provided the closest DMC alternatives for the Anchor colours, but they will not be quite the same. Some Eterna silks are also used.

DMC		Eterna
210	738	4240
211	739	2730
333	742	100
437	762	3970
451	791	**Anchor**
452	841	110 (DMC 3746)
453	934	
640	935	109 (DMC 155)
702	987	
703	3345	
704	3853	
727	3861	
728		

METHOD

leaves key	
A Eterna 4240	F 3345
B 704	G 935
C 703	H 934
D 702	I Eterna 3970
E 987	

1: Leaves

In this project the leaves are not outlined with split stitch. Fill all the leaves in long and short stitch from the tip down towards the base, using A, B, C, D, E, F, G and H.

Take one strand Eterna silk in I and work a line of split stitch on the right hand side of each leaf to create a shadow.

2: Flower stem

Fill the stem with long and short stitch using A, B, C and D.

3: Bud

Outline each petal with split stitch in D.

Start with the three back petals, using A, B, C and D to fill them with long and short stitch.

Fill the two front petals with long and short stitch, working from the tip towards the base in A, B, C, D, E, F and G.

4: Bud base

Outline the bracts of the bud base with split stitch in B.

Fill the bracts with long and short stitch in A, B, C, D and E.

Work the details in Eterna silk in split stitch or straight stitches, using F.

bud key	
A 791	E 210
B 333	F 211
C Anchor 110	G 762
D Anchor 109	

bud base key	
A 739	D 841
B 738	E 640
C 437	F Eterna 100

petals key	
A 791	E 210
B 333	F 211
C Anchor 110	G 762
D Anchor 109	H Eterna 2730

5: Flower petals

Outline each petal with split stitch in one strand D.

Fill the petals in the order shown with long and short stitch, working from the outside tip down towards the base as follows:

Petal 1
A, B, C, D, E, F, G
Petal 2
A, B, C, D, E, F, G; fill turnover with satin stitch in B
Petal 3
A, B, C, D, E, F, G; fill turnover with satin stitch in B
Petal 4
A, B, C, D, E, F, G

Petal 5
A, B, C, D, E, F, G
Petal 6
A, B, C, D, E, F, G; fill turnover with satin stitch in B

Take one strand of fine silk H and work under the overlaps of each petal with split stitch to create a shadow.

centre key	
A 727	C 742
B 728	D 3853

6: Flower centre

Outline the five stamens with split stitch in A, working from the centre as shown in the first photograph.

Fill each stamen with padded satin stitch using B, C and D. Work shadow lines next to these in D.

Add French knots, using one strand and two twists, in A, B and D at the tips of the stamens.

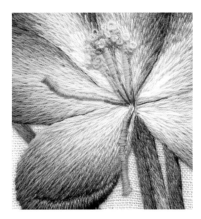

163

Moroccan Plums

Adapted from Morocco plum, Prunus domestica Linnaeus, *Plate 53 in* Hooker's Finest Fruits *by William T. Stearn*

I chose this picture for the deep shades of blue in the fruit.

It would make a good pairing with the orange 'Elton' cherry design

on page 212, as blue and orange are complementary colours.

MATERIALS

white church linen, approx.
30 x 32 cm (12 x 12½ in)

DMC stranded cotton, and
silks, as listed in key

crewel needles sizes 9, 10

frame approx. 27 x 30 cm
(10½ x 12 in) or hoop 25
cm (10 in) diameter

tracing outline
actual size: reduce or enlarge as desired

TBurr 10

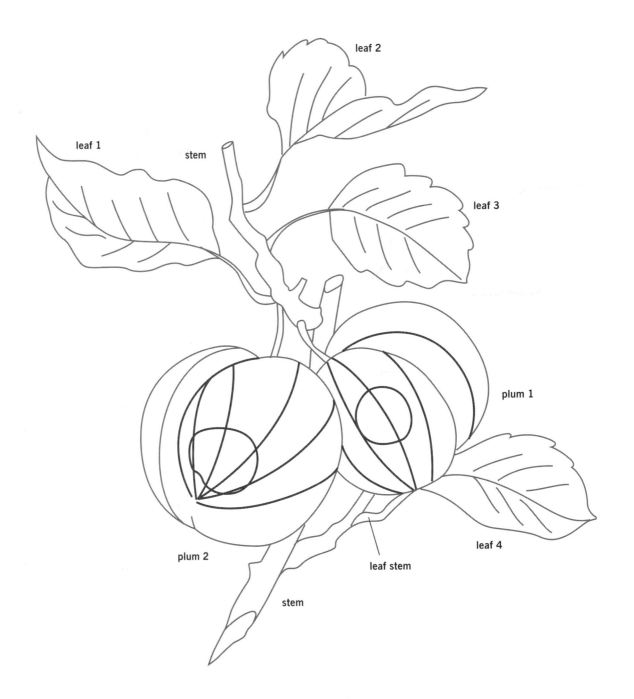

leaf 2

leaf 1

stem

leaf 3

plum 1

plum 2

leaf 4

leaf stem

stem

stitch guide

PREPARATION

Wash and iron the fabric.

Transfer the outline onto the centre of the linen fabric.

Pull a thread at right angles to find the straight grain on both the linen and backing fabric.

Line up the fabrics with the grain and overcast the edges of both pieces of fabric together on a sewing machine or tack by hand.

Mount in hoop or frame ensuring that the fabric is drum tight. You may need to adjust this occasionally as you stitch to keep it taut.

One strand of thread is used throughout this project unless otherwise indicated.

thread key

Anchor and DMC stranded cottons are used in this project.

Anchor	DMC	Eterna
253	434	278
254	436	
266	437	
267	517	
268	738	
842	739	
843	794	
845	801	
862	934	
334	3031	
433	3747	
	3750	
	3842	

METHOD

branch key

A	DMC 739	E	DMC 434
B	DMC 738	F	DMC 433
C	DMC 437	G	DMC 801
D	DMC 436	H	DMC 3031

1: Branch

Fill the branch with long and short stitch, using A, B, C, D, E, F and G.

Add in some straight stitches in H for shadows and notches.

Use the photo as a guide to placing shades.

2: Leaves

Fill all the leaf stems in adjacent rows of split stitch using A, B and C.

Outline all the leaves with split stitch using one strand F.

Fill each leaf with long and short stitch from the outside edge in towards the centre vein as follows:

Leaf 1
top = D, E, F, G
bottom = H, G, F
Leaf 2
top = F, G, H, I
bottom = E, F
Leaf 3
From tip across to base of leaf (both sections) = D, E, F, G, H, I, J
Leaf 4
top = G, F, E
bottom = F, G

leaves key	
A Anchor 842	F Anchor 266
B Anchor 843	G Anchor 267
C Anchor 845	H Anchor 268
D Anchor 253	I Anchor 862
E Anchor 254	J DMC 934

leaf 1

leaf 1

leaf 1

leaf 1

plums key	
A DMC 3747	E DMC 3842
B DMC 794	F DMC 3750
C DMC 334	G Eterna 278
D DMC 517	

3: Plums

Start with the back plum, 1. Outline with split stitch using two strands E.

Fill the back area with long and short stitch from the base up towards the top, using G F E D, C, B and A.

You will need to shorten your stitches and work a couple of rows of each stitch to get around the curve. Keep in line with the direction lines.

Next fill the front portion, again using A, B, C, D, E, F and G. The highlight on the plum is placed near the centre, so all stitches need to be worked around this.

Outline the front plum, 2, with split stitch in two strands of E.

Fill the back portion first, and then the front as shown, in long and short stitch using A, B, C, D, E, F and G.

Add a few small straight stitches in G at the little indent at the base of the plum.

Lilac-breasted Roller

Reproduced with permission of Ed Aylmer, South Africa, Lilac Breasted Roller © 2009.
The Lilac-breasted Roller is widely distributed in sub-Saharan Africa. It is about 37 cm (14½ in) long
and has a turquoise-green head with violet and turquoise chest that is easily visible in the bush.

I chose this bird to represent turquoise and jade green

as these colours are prominent in its plumage.

MATERIALS

white church linen or cotton
satin, approx. 30 x 32 cm
(12 x 12½ in)

DMC stranded cotton, and
silks, as listed in key

crewel needles sizes 9, 10

frame approx. 27 x 30 cm
(10½ x 12 in) or hoop 25
cm (10 in) diameter

tracing outline
actual size: reduce or enlarge as desired

TBurr 09

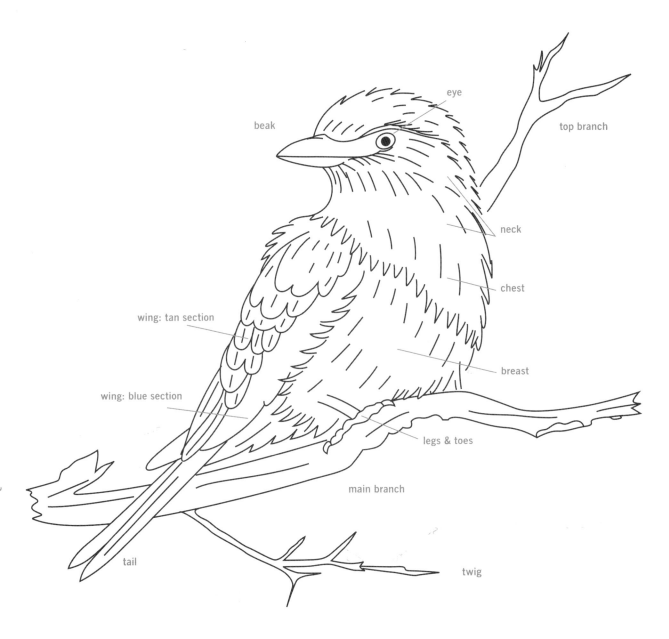

eye

beak

top branch

neck

chest

wing: tan section

breast

wing: blue section

legs & toes

main branch

tail

twig

stitch guide

PREPARATION

Wash and iron the fabric.

Transfer the outline onto the centre of the linen fabric.

Pull a thread at right angles to find the straight grain on both the linen and backing fabric.

Line up the fabrics with the grain and overcast the edges of both pieces of fabric together on a sewing machine or tack by hand.

Mount in hoop or frame ensuring that the fabric is drum tight. You may need to adjust this occasionally as you stitch to keep it taut.

One strand of thread is used throughout this project unless otherwise indicated.

DMC stranded cotton is used in this project.

DMC		
223	758	3765
300	801	3770
301	807	3781
316	844	3799
355	924	3811
356	926	3813
436	928	3817
451	939	3836
502	951	3849
503	3021	3856
598	3023	3860
611	3042	3863
612	3371	3862
613	3768	3864
645	blanc	3865
646	3743	3866
648	3750	
747	3756	

TURQUOISE

METHOD

branches key

A 3866 off-white	G 611 med brown
B 613 pale brown	H 3781 dark brown
C 3864 light rose brown	I 3021 dark grey-brown
D 612 light brown	J 3371 very dark brown
F 3863 med rose brown	

1: Branches

Main branch

Start at the base of the branch as shown.

Work rows of long and short stitch from the outside edge, along the first section of the branch up to the tail, in A, B, C, D, G and H.

Blend the shades into each other and place the lighter shades along the top and the darker shades underneath to create shadows.

Continue filling the branch with A, B, C, D, E, F, G and H as before.

TIP If you find this confusing, try filling the whole branch with shades B, C, D, E and F. Then go back and add highlights with A and shadows with G and H. This can be done by blending in straight stitches on top of the previous ones.

Using I (very dark brown) go back and add random stitches to create notches along the branch.

Top branch

Fill with A, B, C and D. Add shadows with G and notches with H.

Twig

Fill with shades of A, B and C. Add shadows with D and G. This small branch can be filled with rows of split stitch if preferred.

top branch

twig

2: Leg and toes

Fill the leg and toes with satin stitch in A. Blend in a few straight stitches in B.

Add shadows beneath the toes and 'notches' as shown using straight stitches in C.

leg & toes key	
A 3023	C 3021
B 646	

tail key	
A 939	I 502
B 3750	J 3768
C 3765	K 924
D 807	L 844
E 3811	M 3799
F 3849	N 3371
G 3817	O 926
H 928	

2: Tail

Start at the base of the tail and work up the tail in split stitch using A and B.

Work the underneath of the tail in long and short stitch using E, D and C.

Work the two top sections in long and short stitch using H, G and F.

Continue working along the tail and up into the lower body, as shown in the second photograph, in long and short stitch, using the darker shades of I, J and K, and then into the shadows beneath the wing in L, M and N.

When coming up into the lower body start to reverse the shades from N so that they become lighter, as follows: M, L, J and finally O.

Stop filling the body at this stage – you will come back to it later. You need to start on the wings, which are behind the body and breast feathers.

2: Wing: blue section

Fill the underneath area of the wing (on the right next to the breast feathers) with dark shades C and D. The breast feathers will overlap this area later.

Outline each feather segment with B in split stitch.

Start at the base of the feathers near the tail and fill each segment before going onto the next. Fill each segment with long and short stitch, starting from the base towards the top in B, C & D. Make a split stitch line in E to create a cast shadow.

Work the piece that joins the tail in long and short stitch using A, B, C and D.

blue wing section key	
A 3849	D 3799
B 807	E 3371
C 3765	

3: Wing: tan section

Again, start at the base of the feathers near the tail and fill each segment before going onto the next.

Outline each segment in split stitch using B.

Fill the first (lowest) long segment with long and short stitch in B, C, D and E.

Fill all the other segments in B, C and D. Stagger the first row of stitches over the segment to create a feathered look.

At the top of the wing (near the breast) work as one segment only – allow these

tan wing section key	
A 951	D 3862
B 3856	E 3781
C 436	

stitches to become more staggered to create a fluffier feathered look. This area should be worked in rows of long and short stitch in A, B and C. Alternate the shades in each row. Go back and add highlights and shadows by blending in a few straight stitches in A and D where needed

4: Breast

This area is worked as one, not in segments. Continue blending shades from the base up into the chest using A, B, C, D and E. Each row of long and short stitch must overlap the next with staggered stitches to give the effect of feathers.

Start with the deeper shades and work the lighter shades gradually on top of each other, to make the darker shades peep out behind with the lighter shades in front.

Add in a few stitches at the base and against the wing in F. Add in a little A for highlights and G and H for shadows afterwards.

breast key		
A 3756	E 3849
B 747	F 3765
C 598	G 926
D 807	H 3768

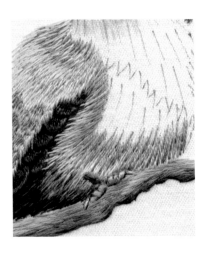

5: Chest

Continue working up from the breast into the chest using shades of A, B, C and D. Blend in a few stitches in E for shadows on the right hand side and into the neck area.

Start blending in a few stitches in F to change from the lilacs to rusts in the neck area.

6: Neck

Continue working from the chest up into the neck, using the previous photograph as a guide. On the right side blend in D, E and F. Towards the left side, and up under the chin, blend in D and B.

Add highlights on top of the stitching as shown, using A and B. Use C to blend the highlights into the chest area.

You will need to work up to the eye and beak. Once the eye and beak are complete you can come back and complete the neck area by bringing the stitches right up to the eye and beak.

chest key		
A 3042		D 451
B 3836		E 3860
C 316		F 223

neck key		
A blanc		D 758
B 3770		E 356
C 3743		F 355

TURQUOISE

eye & beak key	
A 3865	F 3371
B 648	G 301
C 646	H 300
D 645	I 801
E 3021	J 3865

7: Eye and beak

Eye

Outline the bottom and sides of the eye with split stitch in F.

Make a second line close to this in A and another inside this in F.

Fill the bottom of the eye in satin stitch using G, and the top of the eye using H.

Make a few straight stitches for the pupil in F and a small stitch above the pupil in A for the highlight.

Beak

Fill the beak with long and short stitch using B, C, D and E. Go back and blend in the shadows with F. Make a straight line in split stitch across the centre of the beak in F.

The shadows in E and F need to continue up to the eye and around the top of the eye. Lastly take I, and blend this in from the shadows into the rust area on the cheek.

Go back and complete the neck and cheek area by blending the stitches right up to the beak and eye.

8: Head

Starting at the back of the head with F, work staggered long and short stitches to give the effect of feathers. Continue working rows of long and short in E, D, C, B and finally A.

head key	
A 3865	D 3813
B 3756	E 503
C 928	F 502

Little Green Bee-eater

Adapted from a photograph with permission of Jayanth Sharma of Flickr.com.
The Green Bee-eater, Merops orientalis (also called Little Green Bee-eater), is a member of the bee-eater
family found widely across sub-Saharan Africa and Asia through India to Vietnam.

I chose this attractive little bird because of its bright green plumage.

MATERIALS

white church linen or cotton
satin, approx. 30 x 32 cm
(12 x 12½ in)

DMC stranded cotton, and
silks, as listed in key

crewel needles sizes 9, 10

frame approx. 27 x 30 cm
(10½ x 12 in) or hoop 25
cm (10 in) diameter

tracing outline
actual size: reduce or enlarge as desired

T Burr 10

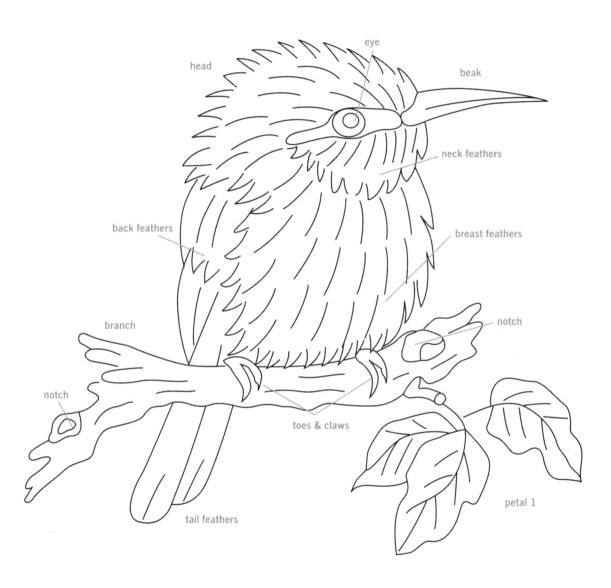

head

eye

beak

neck feathers

back feathers

breast feathers

branch

notch

notch

toes & claws

petal 1

tail feathers

stitch guide

PREPARATION

Wash and iron the fabric.

Transfer the outline onto the centre of the linen fabric.

Pull a thread at right angles to find the straight grain on both the linen and backing fabric.

Line up the fabrics with the grain and overcast the edges of both pieces of fabric together on a sewing machine or tack by hand.

Mount in hoop or frame ensuring that the fabric is drum tight. You may need to adjust this occasionally as you stitch to keep it taut.

thread key

DMC stranded cotton is used in this project.

DMC		
165	703	959
166	704	964
371	728	3021
470	730	3045
471	732	3046
472	783	3047
469	831	3371
581	830	3781
610	898	3787
646	912	3819
648	913	3822
702	936	ecru

One strand of thread is used throughout this project unless otherwise indicated.

METHOD

tail feathers key	
A 371	C 830
B 831	D 3781

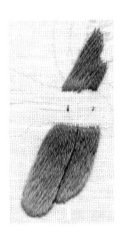

branch key	
A 3047	D 610
B 3046	E 3781
C 3045	F 3021

1: Tail feathers

The tail feathers are not outlined with split stitch.

Fill each section, above and below the branch, from the base up with long and short stitch using A, B, C and D.

2: Branch

Fill the branch with long and short stitch from the outside edge, along its length, leaving spaces for the bird's feet.

Start at the left hand end as shown, using A and B (first photograph).

Continue blending in B, C and D.

Continue blending in A, B, C, D and E.

Fill the little notches at left and right with satin stitch, using A and D. Work all the details and shadows in F.

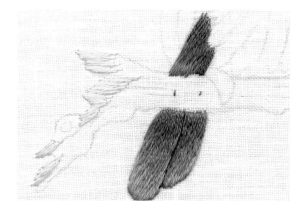

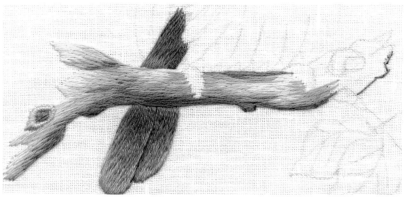

branches and
notches

leaves key	
A 472	D 469
B 471	E 936
C 470	

3: Leaves

Outline each leaf with split stitch in C.

Fill both sides of the centre vein, in long and short stitch, from the outside edge in towards the centre using A, B, C and D.

Work the centre vein in split stitch using E.

Work the leaf stems in split stitch using B and D.

back feathers key	
A 581	C 730
B 732	D 830

4: Back feathers

Fill each section with long and short stitch, starting at the base and working upwards in each section, using A, B, C and D.

5: Breast feathers

Start at the base of the bird's breast and work up towards the chest.

Work a row in A, then blend in another row in B. Blend in and encroach on top of this in C.

Blend in the next two shades, D and E.

Start to blend in the lime green shades, F, G and H, but not in solid rows – you want them to be scattered among the greens.

Change to the deeper shades of green, E and D, towards the neck.

breast feathers key	
A 732	E 704
B 581	F 166
C 702	G 3819
D 703	H 165

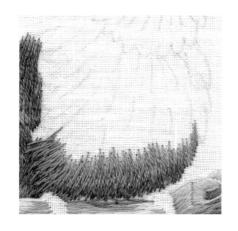

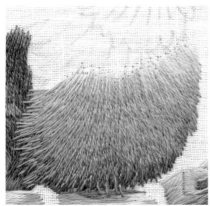
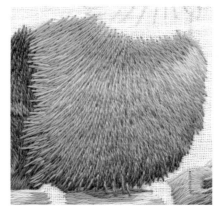

neck feathers key

A	912	D	964
B	913	E	3021
C	959		

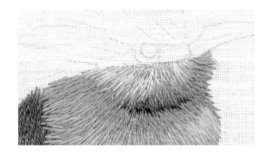

eye key

A	898	D	ecru
B	3371	E	3021
C	648		

beak key

A	648	D	3021
B	646	E	3371
C	3787		

6: Neck feathers

Blend in the neck feathers from the breast, using A, B, C and D.

Blend in a few small stitches at the base of the neck in E to create the dark band.

7: Eye

Work a circle around the pupil in split stitch in A.

Fill the pupil with satin stitch in B.

Make two tiny stitches in D at the top of the pupil for the highlight.

Make a small line of split stitch in C at the base of the eye. Fill the outside of the eye in long and short using B and E.

8: Beak

Start at the base of the upper section of the beak, filling with long and short stitch in A, B, C and D.

Then fill the lower beak with D and E, again starting at the base of the beak.

9: Head

Start at the back of the head and work irregular long and short stitches in towards the beak, using A and B.

Continue filling in the head, using B, C and D, and finally a bit of E above the eye and beak.

head key			
A	3822	D	3819
B	728	E	704
C	783		

9: Toes and claws

It is best to take your fabric out of the hoop to work the bullions for the toes.

Work three small bullions next to each other for each foot as shown, using two strands of A and approximately 8–10 twists so that the bullions lie loosely on the fabric.

Using one strand B, make straight stitches for the claws.

toes & claws key	
A 646	B 3021

Little Bee-eater Friends

This is a simplified version of an earlier bee-eater picture, which I have reproduced due to popular request. The little bee-eater is resident in much of sub-Saharan Africa. It is the smallest bee-eater, about 15 cm (6 in) long, with a green back and head and orange/gold underparts. They are commonly found in pairs or as numerous birds lined up on branches, typically snuggled up together.

I chose these birds because the colour gold is so obvious in its plumage.

tracing outline
reduce/enlarge to desired size

MATERIALS

white church linen or cotton satin, approx. 30 x 32 cm (12 x 12½ in)

DMC stranded cotton, and silks, as listed in key

crewel needles sizes 9, 10

frame approx. 27 x 30 cm (10½ x 12 in) or hoop 25 cm (10 in) diameter

TBurt 10

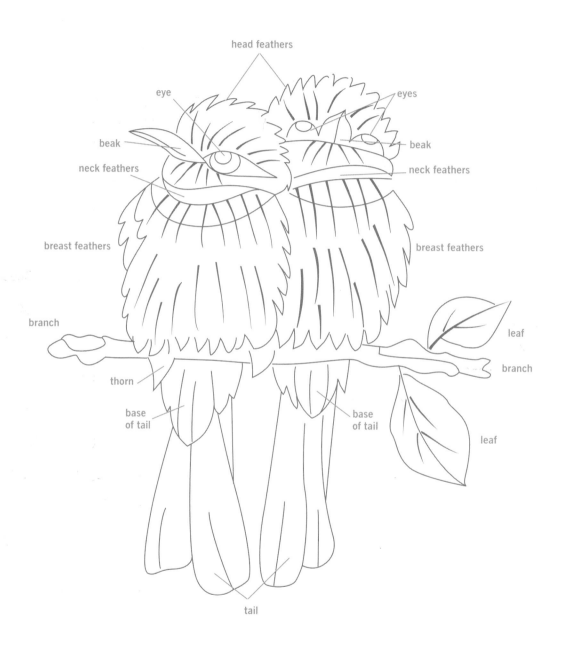

head feathers

eye

eyes

beak

beak

neck feathers

neck feathers

breast feathers

breast feathers

branch

leaf

branch

thorn

base
of tail

base
of tail

leaf

tail

stitch guide

PREPARATION

Wash and iron the fabric.

Transfer the outline onto the centre of the linen fabric.

Pull a thread at right angles to find the straight grain on both the linen and backing fabric.

Line up the fabrics with the grain and overcast the edges of both pieces of fabric together on a sewing machine or tack by hand.

Mount in hoop or frame ensuring that the fabric is drum tight. You may need to adjust this occasionally as you stitch to keep it taut.

thread key

DMC stranded cotton is used in this project.

DMC		
301	727	3011
420	729	3012
422	782	3013
470	801	3021
471	830	3078
472	831	3346
646	832	3371
647	840	3781
648	841	3787
676	842	3821
725	920	3828
726	935	

GOLD

One strand of thread is used throughout this project unless otherwise indicated.

METHOD

tail feathers key	
A 3371	D 841
B 3781	E 842
C 840	

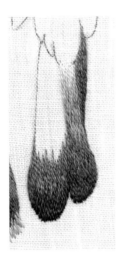
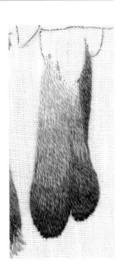

base of tail key	
A 676	C 3828
B 422	D 420

1: Tail feathers and base of tail

Work each tail in the same manner.

Start with the small dark sections at the right back of each tail, filling with long and short stitch in A.

Next work the outer feathers. Fill with long and short stitch from the tips of the feathers upwards, using A, B, C, D and E. Then work the inner (front) feathers in the same way.

Add small straight stitches in at the tips of the tail feathers in E and D.

Next work the bases of the tails (just below the branch), filling with long and short stitch, using A, B, C and D.

2: Branch

Start out the ends of the branch and work in towards the centre. Fill with long and short stitch using A, B, C, D and E.

The lighter shades will be concentrated on the ends of the branch and the darker shades in the centre section, which will later be partially covered by feathers.

Fill the two thorns with straight stitches in B and C.

Outline the details and emphasise the shadows using one strand F

branch key	
A 842	D 3781
B 841	E 3021
C 840	

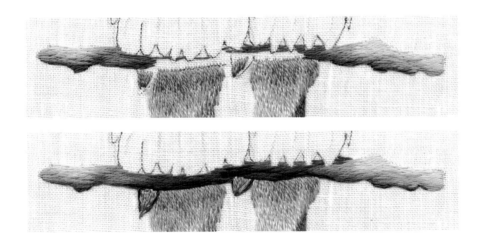

breast feathers key	
A 420	H 782
B 830	I 301
C 831	J 920
D 832	K 3021
E 729	L 3371
F 3821	M 646
G 729	

3: Breast feathers

The breast feathers for both birds are worked in the same manner and in the same shades.

Start at the base and work up towards the neck. The base feathers should overlap onto the branch.

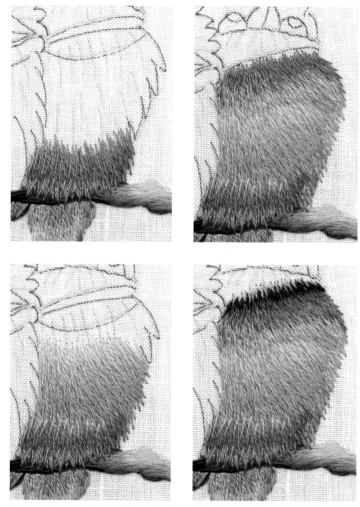

Photographs show the working of the breast feathers for the bird on the right.

Fill with irregular long and short stitch from the base up towards the neck.

Start with A, B and C.

Continue blending with D, E and F.

Continue blending with G, H, I and J until you reach the neck area.

For the band at the base of the neck blend in small straight stitches in K and L. Finally add a few stitches in M in preparation for the lighter shades on the neck.

4: Neck feathers

The neck feathers for both birds are worked in the same manner and in the same shades.

Use the photograph of the finished project to adjust placement for the bird on the left.

Continue blending with A, B, C and D from the breast feathers into the neck, using irregular long and short stitches.

When you have completed the eye and beak go back and add in a few tiny straight stitches to soften the line.

neck feathers key	
A 3078	C 726
B 727	D 725

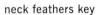

beak key		
Bird on right		*Bird on left*
A 842		A 647
B 840		B 646
C 3787		C 3787
D 3371		D 3021
		E 3371

5: Beaks

Bird on right

Fill the beak with long and short stitch from the tip towards the base using A, B, C and D.

Bird on left

Fill the top portion of the beak first, using A, B, C and D. Fill the bottom portion of the beak using D and E.

eyes key	
A 648	C 3371
B 801	D 3021

6: Eyes

Use the step-by-step photos as a guide to working all the eyes.

Outline the pupil with satin stitches using B.

Fill the pupil with satin stitches using C. Outline the eye and surrounding area with split stitch in C.

Make two tiny stitches at the top of the pupil in A for the highlight. Make a thin line of split stitch across the bottom of the eye in A.

Fill the outer area of the eye in long and short stitch in C and D to complete.

7: Head feathers

Work the head feathers for both birds in the same manner. Start at the outside edge of the head and work irregular long and short stitches in towards the beak and eyes.

Start with A and B. Continue blending with C and D until the head is filled. Go back and add in a few highlights of A as shown.

head feathers key	
A 472	C 470
B 471	D 3346

7: Leaves

Outline the large leaf with split stitch. Fill on either side of the centre vein with long and short stitch from the outside e in towards the centre vein using C and D on the left side, and A, B and C on the right side.

Fill the smaller leaf with A and C on the left side, and C and D on the right side.

Work the centre veins in D.

leaves key	
A 3013	C 3011
B 3012	D 935

When you have finished stitching, cast a critical eye over your work and add more highlights and shadows if you think they are necessary.

Austrian Rose

Adapted from Rosa eglanteria, *Yellow Austrian Rose, by Pierre-Joseph Redouté.*

I chose this pretty single rose to represent soft shades of yellow.

MATERIALS

off-white linen or cotton satin, approx. 30 x 32 cm (12 x 12½ in)

fine batiste for backing, approx. 30 x 32 cm (12 x 12½ in) (optional)

DMC stranded cotton, and silks, as listed in key

crewel needles sizes 9, 10

frame approx. 27 x 30 cm (10½ x 12 in) or hoop 25 cm (10 in) diameter

tracing outline
actual size: reduce or enlarge as desired

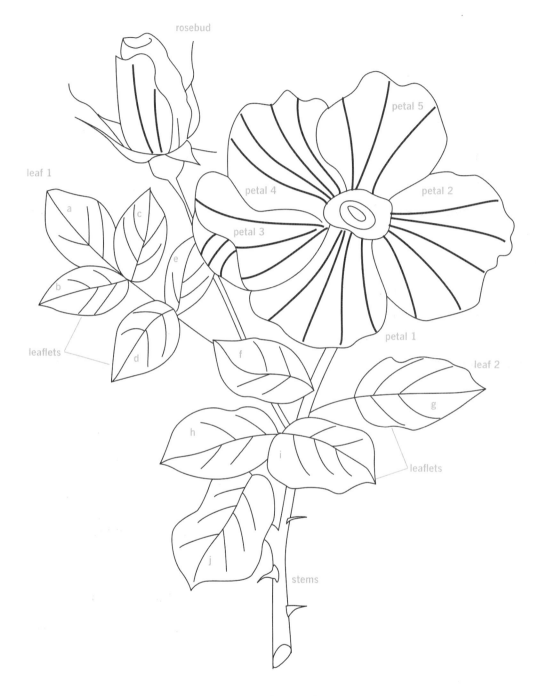

rosebud

petal 5

leaf 1

petal 4

petal 2

a

c

petal 3

e

b

leaflets

d

petal 1

f

leaf 2

g

h

i

leaflets

j

stems

stitch guide

PREPARATION

Wash and iron the fabric.

Transfer the outline onto the centre of the linen fabric.

Pull a thread at right angles to find the straight grain on both the linen and backing fabric.

Line up the fabrics with the grain and overcast the edges of both pieces of fabric together on a sewing machine or tack by hand.

Mount in hoop or frame ensuring that the fabric is drum tight. You may need to adjust this occasionally as you stitch to keep it taut.

One strand of thread is used throughout this project unless otherwise indicated.

thread key

DMC and Anchor stranded cottons are used in this project. DMC alternatives to the Anchor colours are provided in brackets although they will not be the same. Some Eterna silks are also used.

DMC		Anchor
167	934	681 (DMC 3051)
524	936	
640	3045	846 (DMC 935)
727	3078	
728	3011	842 (DMC 3013)
730	3012	
732	3013	**Eterna**
733	3052	1440
780	3053	3970
781	3820	4620
783	3821	4460
840	3822	
841	3823	
842	3866	

YELLOW

METHOD

stems key	
A 3866	F 3013
B 842	G 3012
C 841	H 640
D 840	I Eterna 1440
E 524	

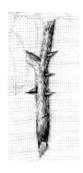 

1: Stem

Main stem

Fill the stem with adjacent rows of split stitch shading across from left to right in A, B, C and D.

Add a few straight stitches at the base in E.

Add thorns and shadows with one strand fine silk in I.

Upper stems

Fill each stem with adjacent rows of split stitch shading with E, F, G and H.

Add thorns and shadows with one strand fine silk in I.

rosebud key	
A 3013	I 783
B 3012	J 781
C 3011	K 780
D 936	L 3823
E Eterna 4460	M 3078
F 3822	N 727
G 3821	O 3045
H 3820	P Eterna 4620

2: Rosebud

Start with the sepals and base-– fill with long and short stitch using A, B, C and D.

Add fine details in silk E.

Next work the back part of the bud. Outline with split stitch using one strand of F. Fill with long and short stitch from the outside edge in towards the base in F, G, H, I, J and K.

Add a small shadow at the tip with O.

Outline the front part of the bud with split stitch, using one strand F. Fill with long and short stitch from the outside edge in towards the base in L, M, N, F and G.

Add shadows to the base of the rosebud with silk in P.

3: Leaves

Leaf 1

Outline each of the five leaflets with split stitch in B. Fill with long and short stitch from the outside edge in towards the centre vein, working from the tip of the leaflet towards the base.

Leaflet a
left side = A, B, C, D
right side = A, B, C, D
Leaflet b
upper side = A, B, C, D
lower side =B, C, D
Leaflet c
left side = A, B, C, D
right side =A, B, C, D
Leaflet d
left side = A, B, C
right side = B, C, D
Leaflet e
left side = A
right side = C, D

leaf 1 key	
A 733	C 730
B 732	D 936

YELLOW

leaf 2 key			
A	Anchor 842	E	Anchor 682
B	3053	F	934
C	3052	G	Eterna 3970
D	Anchor 681		

rose petals key			
A	3823	E	3821
B	3078	F	728
C	727	G	Eterna 4620
D	3822		

Leaf 2

Outline each of the five leaflets with split stitch in B. Fill with long and short stitch from the outside edge in towards the centre vein, working from the tip of the leaflet towards the base.

Leaflet f
lower side = A, B, C, D, E
upper side = A, B, C, D, E
Leaflet g
lower side = F, E, D
upper side = B, C, D
Leaflet h
lower side = C, D, E, F
upper side = A, B, C, D, E, F
Leaflet i
lower side = A, B, C, D, E
upper side =A, B, C, D, E
Leaflet j
left side = A, B, C, D, E, F
right side = A, B, C, D, E, F

Go back and add in details with fine silk G. Stitch tiny straight stitches at the edges of the leaves and for veins as shown. Work centre veins in split stitch in F.

4: Rose petals

Use the photographs as a guide to the placement of colours.

Outline each petal first in split stitch in B.

Fill each petal with long and short stitch from the outside edge in towards the centre.

Petal 1
A, B, C, D, E, F
Petal 2
A, B, C, D, E, F
Petal 3
A, B, C, D, E; outline and pad the turnover as shown with A; fill with satin stitch in A and then add a few straight stitches at the base of the turnover in D.
Petal 4
A, B, C, D, E, F
Petal 5
A, B, C, D, E, F

Take one strand of fine silk G and add shadows under the overlap of each petal.

petal 1

petal 2

petal 3

petal 4

petal 5

5: Flower centre

Fill the centre with French knots, using one strand and two twists, in A and B.

Around this make straight stitches from the centre outwards in B, C and D.

Work clusters of French knots at the tips of the straight stitches in A, B, C and D.

flower centre key		
A 3078		C 167
B 3822		D 728

'Elton' Cherry

Adapted from Elton Cherry, Prunus avium Linnaeus, *Plate XX in Hooker's Finest Fruits by William T. Stearn.*

I chose these large and beautiful cherries to represent the colour orange. Despite their colouring they are classified as white cherries rather than black, and are commonly regarded as the standard for dessert quality.

MATERIALS
off-white linen or cotton satin, approx. 30 x 32 cm (12 x 12½ in)

DMC stranded cotton, and silks, as listed in key

crewel needles sizes 9, 10

frame approx 27 x 30 cm (10½ x 12 in) or hoop 25 cm (10 in) diameter

tracing outline
actual size: reduce or enlarge as desired

TBurr 10

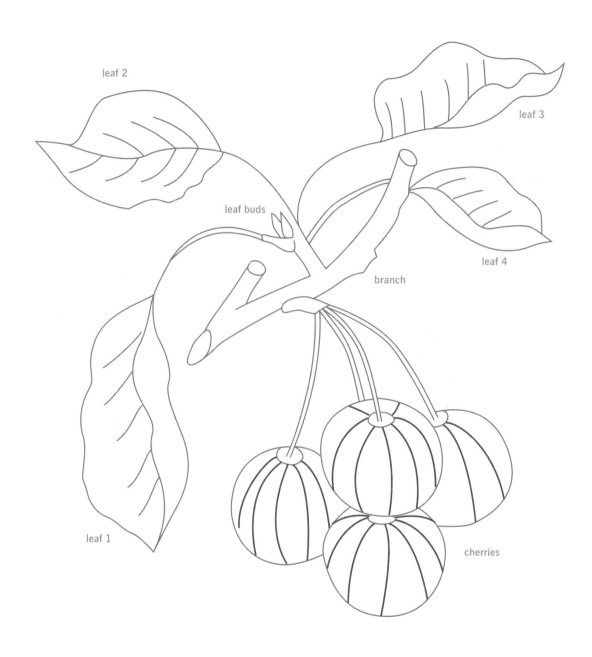

leaf 2

leaf 3

leaf buds

leaf 4

branch

leaf 1

cherries

stitch guide

PREPARATION

Wash and iron the fabric.

Transfer the outline onto the centre of the linen fabric.

Pull a thread at right angles to find the straight grain on both the linen and backing fabric.

Line up the fabrics with the grain and overcast the edges of both pieces of fabric together on a sewing machine or tack by hand.

Mount in hoop or frame ensuring that the fabric is drum tight. You may need to adjust this occasionally as you stitch to keep it taut.

thread key
DMC stranded cottons are used in this project.

DMC		
165	720	934
420	721	3012
433	740	3045
435	742	3046
469	743	3047
470	869	3051
471	918	3781
472	920	

One strand of thread is used throughout this project unless otherwise indicated.

ORANGE

METHOD

branch key

A	3047	E	869
B	3046	F	3781
C	3045	G	165
D	420	H	3012

leaves & leaf stems key

A	3047	F	470
B	435	G	469
C	433	H	3051
D	472	I	934
E	471		

1: Branch

Fill the branch with long and short stitch along its length, using B, C, D, E and F.

Fill the three cut ends with A and G.

Fill the little leaf buds with straight stitches in G and H.

Leaves and leaf stems

Fill the leaf stems with adjacent rows of split stitch in A, B and C.

Outline each leaf with split stitch using two strands F.

Fill on each leaf with long and short stitch.

Leaf 1
left side = D, E, F, G, H, I
right side = D, F

Leaf 2

upper side = D, E, F, G

lower side = G, H, I

Leaf 3

upper side = E, F, G, H, I

lower side = E, F

Leaf 4

upper side = D, E, F, G

lower side = D, E

Work the centre veins in split stitch in I.

leaf 3

leaf 2

leaf 4

leaf 1

cherries key	
A 743	F 920
B 742	G 918
C 740	H 3781
D 721	I 165
E 720	J 3012

3: Cherries

Outline the cherries with split stitch using two strands C.

Fill each cherry with long and short stitch. Start at the base of the cherry and work up towards the stem indent, carefully following the guidelines to maintain the round shape. You will need to shorten your stitches and work more than one row of each colour to get around the curve.

Use A, B, C, D, E, F and G.

Fill the stem indent with straight stitches in H.

When all the cherries are complete, work the stems, filling them with adjacent rows of split stitch in I and J.

TBurr 10

Tufted Flycatcher

Adapted with permission from a photograph by Lubos Mraz, NaturePhoto.com.

This little bird, which I have chosen to represent the colour brown, is native to Mexico, Ecuador and Peru, although rare vagrants have been sighted in Texas.

MATERIALS

white linen or cotton satin, approx. 30 x 32 cm (12 x 12½ in)

DMC stranded cotton, and silks, as listed in key

crewel needles sizes 9, 10

frame approx 27 x 30 cm (10½ x 12 in) or hoop 25 cm (10 in) diameter

tracing outline
actual size: reduce or enlarge as desired

TBurr 10

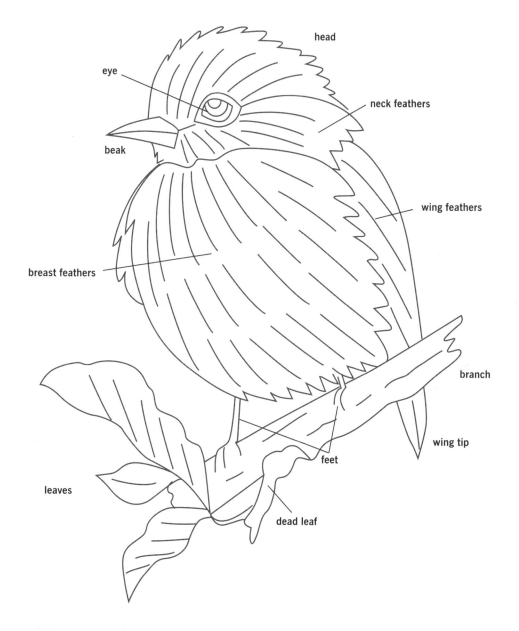

head

eye

neck feathers

beak

wing feathers

breast feathers

branch

wing tip

feet

leaves

dead leaf

stitch guide

PREPARATION

Wash and iron the fabric.

Transfer the outline onto the centre of the linen fabric.

Pull a thread at right angles to find the straight grain on both the linen and backing fabric.

Line up the fabrics with the grain and overcast the edges of both pieces of fabric together on a sewing machine or tack by hand.

Mount in hoop or frame ensuring that the fabric is drum tight. You may need to adjust this occasionally as you stitch to keep it taut.

thread key

DMC stranded cottons are used in this project.

DMC		
420	644	3013
435	646	3021
436	712	3032
437	738	3363
520	739	3371
522	801	3781
524	839	3790
610	840	3827
612	3012	3863

One strand of thread is used throughout this project unless otherwise indicated.

BROWN

METHOD

branch key	
A 644	D 840
B 3032	E 839
C 3863	

1: Branch

Working from left to right, fill the branch with long and short stitch, using A, B, C, D and E.

Use the darker shades – C, D, E – in the centre of the branch to create a shadow.

Work the stem of the dead leaf curling back against the branch in split stitch with B and C, and embroider the leaf itself in long and short stitch in B, C, D and E.

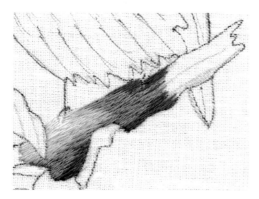

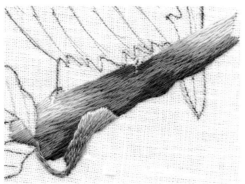

feet key	
A 646	B 3021

2: Feet

Take the fabric out of the hoop to work the bullions for the bird's feet.

First work the legs in adjacent lines of split stitch using A and B.

Work the right foot in two bullions next to each other using 1 strand and 8 twists in A.

Work the left foot in three bullions next to each other using 1 strand and 8 twists for the two toes on the left, and 12 twists for the toe on the right, in A.

Make straight stitches for the claws in B.

Return the fabric to the hoop.

3: Leaves

Outline each leaf with split stitch in a medium shade of green such as C or D.

Fill each leaf with long and short stitch from the outside edge in towards the centre.

Work the bottom leaf in B, C and D.

Work the upper side of the small middle leaf in A, F and E, and the lower side in E. Fill the centre vein with split stitch in E.

Work the large upper leaf in A, B, C, D and E.

leaves key	
A 524	D 3363
B 3013	E 520
C 3012	F 522

wing feathers key		
A 3032		C 3781
B 3790		D 3021

4: Wing feathers

Start with the wing-tip below the branch – fill with long and short stitch in C and D.

Fill the wing feathers with long and short stitch, shading with D, C, B, A, B, C and D up to the neck.

Fill the small section of wing on the left side of the bird with long and short stitch using C and D.

breast feathers key		
A 610		F 437
B 420		G 738
C 435		H 739
D 436		I 712
E 3827		

5: Breast feathers

Start at the base of the breast and work up towards the neck. Fill with irregular long and short stitch using A, B and C. Work two rows of each shade.

Continue, blending in D, E and F. Again, work two rows of each shade, staggering the stitches into each row.

Continue blending with two or three rows each of G, H and I. Finally blend in H and some G, up to and encroaching slightly into, the neck area.

226

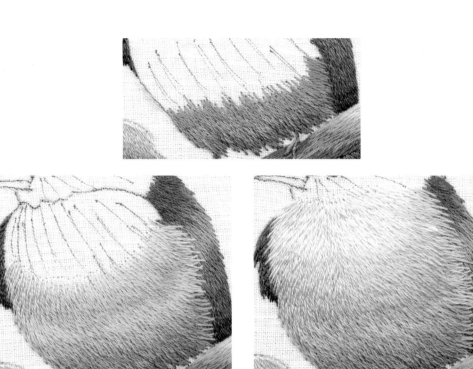

breast feathers

6: Eye

Fill the pupil with satin stitch in C.

Fill the iris around the pupil with satin stitch in B.

Make two tiny stitches at the top of the pupil in A for the highlights.

Work a line of split stitch in C along the base of the iris.

Work a line of split stitch in A below this.

Stitch a line of split stitch in D around the whole eye.

eye key	
A 644	C 3371
B 801	D 3021

beak key	
A 644	C 3790
B 3032	D 3021

7: Beak

Fill the bottom half of the beak with long and short stitch in D and C.

Fill the top half with long and short stitch in A, B and C.

neck feathers key	
A 712	E 436
B 739	F 612
C 738	G 610
D 437	

8: Neck feathers

Continue blending up from the breast feathers into the neck feathers. Work from the back in towards the beak and eye in irregular long and short stitch, using A, B, C, D, E, F and G.

BROWN PROJECT: *Tufted Flycatcher*

9: Head

Continue blending from the neck up into the head. Work from the back of the head towards the eye and beak in irregular long and short stitch, using A, B, C, D, E, F and G. The darker shades – D, E, F, G – will be at the front of the head, closer to the beak. Note how the feathers in the bird's crest open slightly to achieve the 'tufted' appearance referred to in the bird's name.

head key		
A 739		E 612
B 738		F 3032
C 437		G 610
D 436		

Camellia 'Alba Plena'

Adapted from Camellia japonica *'Alba Plena', Camellia fleurs blanches, by Pierre-Joseph Redouté.*

I chose this camellia to represent the colour white,

which has innumerable variations.

MATERIALS

white linen or cotton satin, approx. 30 x 32 cm (12 x 12½ in)

DMC stranded cotton, and silks, as listed in key

crewel needles sizes 9, 10

frame approx 27 x 30 cm (10½ x 12 in) or hoop 25 cm (10 in) diameter

tracing outline
reduce/enlarge to desired size

TBurr 10

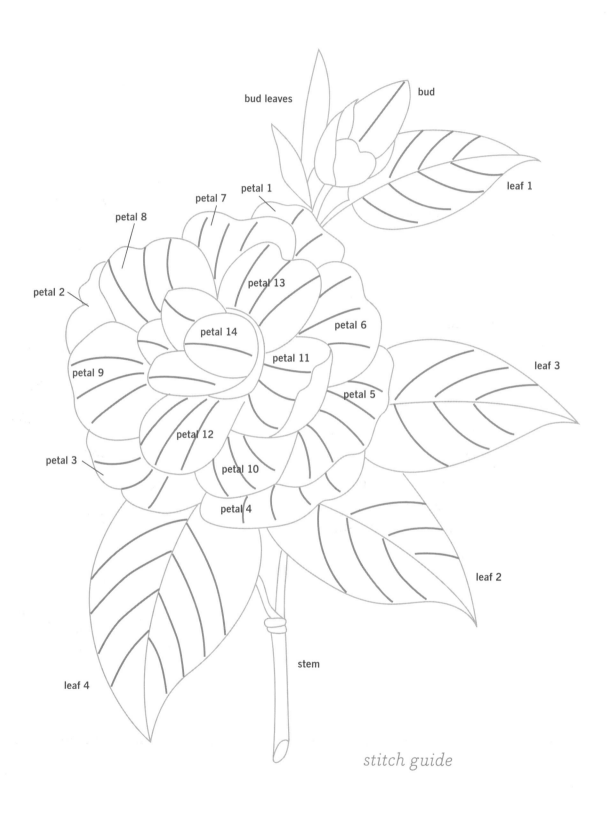

bud leaves

bud

leaf 1

petal 1

petal 7

petal 8

petal 13

petal 2

petal 14

petal 6

petal 9

petal 11

leaf 3

petal 5

petal 12

petal 3

petal 10

petal 4

leaf 2

leaf 4

stem

stitch guide

PREPARATION

Wash and iron the fabric.

Transfer the outline onto the centre of the linen fabric.

Pull a thread at right angles to find the straight grain on both the linen and backing fabric.

Line up the fabrics with the grain and overcast the edges of both pieces of fabric together on a sewing machine or tack by hand.

Mount in hoop or frame ensuring that the fabric is drum tight. You may need to adjust this occasionally as you stitch to keep it taut.

One strand of thread is used throughout this project unless otherwise indicated.

METHOD

stems key

A 834	E 838
B 832	F 733
C 830	G 732
D 378	

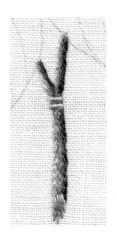

1: Stems

Fill the stems with adjacent rows of split stitch, using A, B, C, D and E.

At the base work a few straight stitches in F and G.

The notches should be worked across in padded satin stitch in A, with a few straight lines between them in C.

bud & leaves key

A 733	H 471
B 732	I 3347
C 730	J blanc
D 935	K 3865
E 830	L ecru
F 772	M 644
G 472	N 524

2: Bud & leaves

Work the bud and leaf stems first in split stitch, using B, C and E.

Outline each bud leaf with split stitch in A. Fill the leaves with padding, using straight stitches across the leaf in A.

Fill each leaf on top of the padding with long and short stitch, shading from top to bottom in A, B, C and D.

Fill the bud with long and short stitch, shading with J, K, L, M and N. Make sure that the lighter shades are on the left side and darker shades on the right.

Fill the sepals of the bud base with long and short stitch in F, G, H and I.

3: Leaves

Outline each leaf with split stitch in D.

Fill on either side of the centre vein with long and short stitch from the outside in towards the vein. Keep in line with the pencil guidelines.

Leaf 1
upper side = H, I
lower side = F, G, H, I
Leaf 2
left side =F, E, D, C, B
right side = F, E, D, C, B, A

leaves key	
A Eterna 4290	F 3346
B 472	G 3345
C 471	H 319
D 470	I 934
E 469	

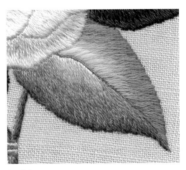

leaf 1

leaf 2

leaf 3

leaf 4

Leaf 3

upper side = D, E, F, G, H, I

lower side = D, E, F, G, H, I

Leaf 4

left side = D, E, F, G, H

right side = I, H, G, F, E

Work the centre veins in split stitch using one strand I plus one strand of D next to this.

4: Camellia flower

Each petal is numbered, from 1 to 14.

Starting with the back petals and working forward, outline each petal with split stitch in F.

Fill each petal with long and short stitch from the outside edge in towards the centre.

Petal 1: A, B, C
Petal 2: A, B, C
Petal 3: A, D, B, C
Petal 4: A, D, C
Petal 5: E, F, G, H, I
Petal 6: E, F, G, H, I, C
Petal 7: E, F, G, H, I
Petal 8: E, F, G, J
Petal 9: E, G, I
Petal 10: E, G, I
Petal 11: E, G, H; *turnover:* G
Petal 12: H, G, F, E
Petal 13: E, F, G, J
Petal 14 (centre petals): E, F, G, B

Enhance the shadows with a few straight stitches in K.

flower key	
A 762	G ecru
B 648	H 644
C 647	I 524
D 3024	J Eterna 4023
E blanc	K Eterna 4290
F 3865	L Eterna 150

Sacred Kingfisher

This painting by Christopher Pope was made into a postage stamp for Australia Post. Reproduced here by permission of Christopher Pope, 2009.

This is an inspirational project, representing the colours blue, yellow and gold, included to challenge more advanced stitchers. The Sacred Kingfisher is a medium sized kingfisher found in Australia, New Zealand and Indonesia.

MATERIALS
white linen/cotton satin, approx. 30 x 32 cm (12 x 12½ in)

DMC stranded cotton, and silks, as listed in key

crewel needles sizes 9, 10

frame approx 27 x 30 cm (10½ x 12 in) or hoop 25 cm (10 in) diameter

tracing outline
actual size: reduce or enlarge as desired

The original painting is acrylic on board painted in 1997 and sold to a family friend. The size is h12" x w14" [30 x 35.5 cm].
Kingfishers are one of my favourite birds to paint – and I have painted a few. CHRISTOPHER POPE

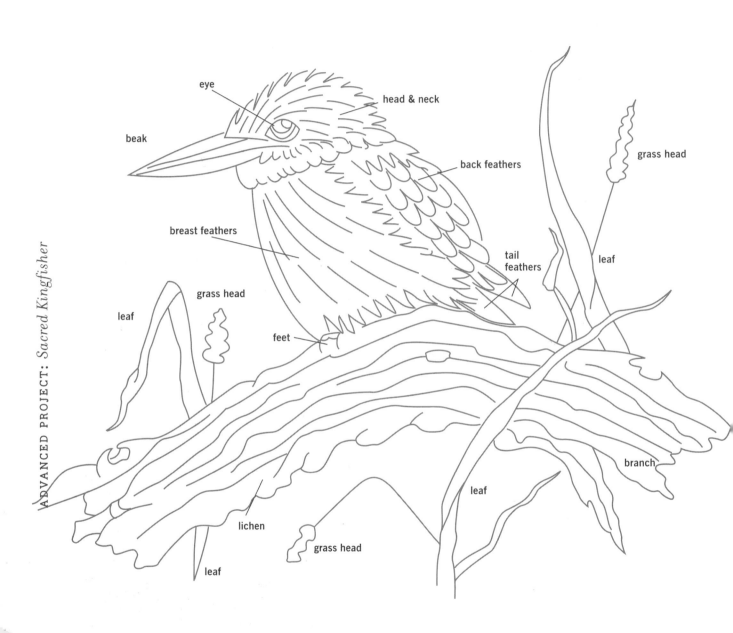

eye

head & neck

beak

back feathers

grass head

breast feathers

tail feathers

leaf

grass head

feet

leaf

branch

leaf

lichen

leaf

grass head

stitch guide

PREPARATION

Wash and iron the fabric.

Transfer the outline onto the centre of the linen fabric.

Pull a thread at right angles to find the straight grain on both the linen and backing fabric.

Line up the fabrics with the grain and overcast the edges of both pieces of fabric together on a sewing machine or tack by hand.

Mount in hoop or frame ensuring that the fabric is drum tight. You may need to adjust this occasionally as you stitch to keep it taut.

One strand of thread is used throughout this project unless otherwise indicated.

thread key

DMC stranded cotton and Eterna silk are used in this project.

DMC			
162	642	813	3053
165	644	823	3078
168	645	825	3371
169	646	826	3756
310	647	827	3781
370	648	833	3782
336	676	844	3787
369	680	898	3799
413	727	931	3822
433	739	932	3862
610	746	3047	3864
611	779	3012	3865
612	813	3047	3866
613	803	3013	blanc

Eterna		
202S	208S	300S
4620S	278S	310S
110S	4350S	320S

METHOD

branch key	
A 3866	G 739
B 644	H 3782
C 648	I 642
D 647	J 3787
E 646	K 844
F 645	L Eterna 202S

1: Branch

If you find yourself daunted by the number of colours and want to simplify the shading on the branch, you can cut down the colours to A, C, D, E, F, K and L. It will not give such a lifelike result but will create a similar effect.

Work the branch in sections – start on the left as shown and fill the top sections (lighter areas) with long and short stitch using A, B, C, D, E, G, H and I. Use the pictures as a guide to placing the lighter shades.

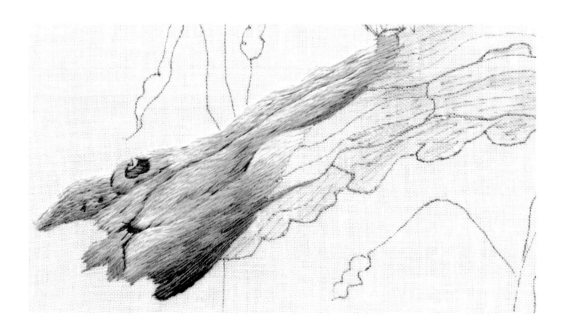

244

The light source is at top left, so everything in that area will be lighter and everything on the bottom right will be shadowed and darker.

Blend in the lower sections (areas in shadow) of the branch with E, F, J and K. Finally, take one strand of silk L to add the fine details – notches and small lines – in straight stitches.

Continue working along the branch in sections. Note the shadowed area underneath the bird, and the positions of the lighter areas. It may help to sketch these in with a pencil or permanent micron pen before stitching.

Add in all the details (notches and lines) when the long and short stitching is complete, using one strand of silk L.

lichen key			
A	932	C	844
B	931	D	369

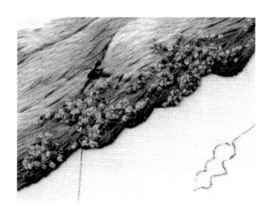

2: Lichen

The lichen along the underside of the branch is portrayed with tiny French knots (one strand and one twist), using a mixture of A, B, C and D.

leaves key			
A	3047	F	370
B	165	G	611
C	3013	H	3781
D	3053	I	Eterna 4620S
E	3012	J	Eterna 110S

3: Leaves

Fill each leaf with long and short stitch, starting from the base of the leaf and working up towards the tip, using A, B, C, D, E and F.

Add shadows afterwards by blending in a few straight stitches in G and H.

Add details using one strand fine silk in I and J.

4: Grass heads

Fill the grass stems with adjacent rows of split stitch using A, B, C, D and E.

Fill the grass heads with a mix of French knots using a combination of two strands together in the needle:

A + B (3047 + 613)
A +D (3047 + 3053)
D + C (3053 + 612)
C + E (612 + 611)
2 strands of F (3781)

Start with the lighter shades and work across from the left, scattering the knots into each other. Finish with a few knots in the darker shades to create shadows.

grass heads key	
A 3047	D 3053
B 613	E 611
C 612	F 3781

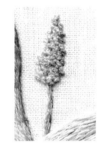 

foot key	
A 648	B 645

5: Foot

Using one strand of A, make a long bullion, approximately 10 twists, for the long toe. Make a smaller one close to this. Under the toe work a line of split stitch using one strand B.

Work the smaller toe in a shorter bullion, approximately 4 twists, and outline as before.

tail feathers key	
A 813	D 803
B 826	E 823
C 825	F Eterna 208

6: Tail feathers

Outline each feather in split stitch using one strand C.

Fill the lower feather with long and short stitch from the outside edge in towards the base, using A, B, C, D, E and F.

Work the upper feathers as before using E, F, A, B, C and D, being guided by the photograph for colour placement.

7: Wing feathers

Work the darker shades near the breast feathers first, using long and short stitch in I, J, K and L (see the detail picture for guidance).

Next work the small feathers individually. Outline each one in split stitch and fill with long and short stitch at an angle, using E, F, G, H, I and J. The feathers lower down the back are in slightly darker shades and the ones nearer the neck are lighter.

Take one strand of silk M and work a gold outline around the edge of each feather in tiny straight stitches.

Blend in the feathers at the top of the back in long and short stitch using D, C and B, and finally up towards the neck in A.

wing feathers key	
A blanc	I 336
B 3756	J 823
C 162	K Eterna 278
D 827	(charcoal)
E 813	L Eterna 208 (dark
F 826	charcoal)
G 825	M 4350 (gold)
H 803	

breast feathers key	
A 3865	H 612
B 746	I 610
C 3078	J 647
D 727	K 646
E 3822	L Eterna 300
F 676	M Eterna 310
G 613	N Eterna 320

7: Breast feathers

The breast feathers should be worked in staggered long and short stitch (feather stitch) from the bottom of the breast up towards the neck.

Work the darker shades at the base first, in K, I, H and F.

Continue, blending in the lighter shades above this section, using E, D, C, B, and finally A.

Notice that the left side is lighter than the right side. The colours also get lighter the nearer you get to the neck – work these areas in A, B and C, and then G and J for shadows.

Go back afterwards and add a few feathery strokes out onto the back feathers, using the silks L, M and N.

To get the feathers to curve you can make two straight stitches into each other at an angle (red indicates the stitches).

![TIP] You can go back afterwards and add layers of lighter or darker shades where needed. You can work up to three layers and make the stitches go at different angles to get the feathery effect.

9: Eye & beak

Fill the base of the eye with split stitch in C.

Work a line of split stitch above this in B.

Fill the pupil in satin stitch in A and work a line below the eye with split stitch in E. Make a few tiny stitches in D for the highlight. Outline the complete eye in split stitch in A.

Work the lower part of the beak first. Fill with long and short stitch, shading with A, B, C, D and E.

Work the upper part of the beak next. Fill with long and short stitch, shading with F, G, H, B and A. Go back and make a line down the centre of the beak and towards the eye area with A.

eye key	
A 3371	D 3756
B 898	E 3782
C 433	

beak key	
A 310	E 3864
B 3799	F 168
C 779	G 169
D 3862	H 413

head & neck key	
A 827	H 833
B 813	I 680
C 826	J 433
D 825	K 898
E 803	L 3865
F 336	M 645
G 823	

10: Head & neck

Work the head feathers from the outside in towards the eye and beak in long and short stitch, using G, F, E, D, C, B and A.

Add a few straight stitches above the eye and into the beak with H, I, J and K.

Finally, finish the white feathers at the neck in L and blend in a bit of M for shadows.

When your embroidery is completed, examine it critically and add in any desirable detailing with fine Eterna silk.

USEFUL INFORMATION

books & dvd by Trish Burr

Redouté's Finest Flowers in Embroidery

Milner Craft Series, 2006. Seventeen flower projects of Pierre-Joseph Redouté, early nineteenth century botanical artist.

Long & Short Stitch Embroidery: A Collection of Flowers

Milner Craft Series, 2006. Covers all aspects of the technique and includes 21 flower projects.

Crewel & Surface Embroidery: Inspirational Floral Ideas

Milner Craft Series, 2008. Seventeen floral projects using mixed media.

Needle Painting Embroidery: Fresh Ideas for Beginners

Milner Craft Series, 2011. Detailed tutorials on the technique plus 15 projects.

The Long & The Short of It – A DVD Tutorial

Comprehensive tutorials and demonstrations on all aspects of the technique: www.trishburr.co.za

I have found the book by Gail Marsh, *18th Century Embroidery Techniques* (GMC Publications, London, 2006) an extremely useful reference.

suppliers

Trish Burr Embroidery – South Africa

Website: www.trishburr.co.za

Email: erenvale@mweb.co.za

Books, kits, DVD tutorial and pre-printed fabric packs. International shipping available.

Mace & Nairn – UK

Website: www.maceandnairn.com

Email: enquiries@maceandnairn.com

Linen, cotton satin fabric plus full range of DMC and Anchor threads. Wendy is always available to help with your individual needs and ships worldwide.

Thistle Needleworks - USA

Website: www.thistleneedleworks.com

Email: ThisNeedle@aol.com

Linen fabric. Ask for item No 132628 No 401 Linen white. This linen is a milky white and slightly cheaper than church linen.

Please ensure you wash in very hot water to pre-shrink before washing. International shipping available.

Communion Linens - USA

Website: www.communionlinens.com

Email: linens@communionlinens.com

Medium weight Irish linen as used for altar cloths, etc. This is a superb linen, a little pricey but worth the extra cost for the quality. International shipping available.

Marie Suarez – Belgium

Website: www.mariesuarez.com

Email: mariesuarez@skynet.be

This website is in French, but if you email Marie she speaks English and is always willing to cater for your individual needs.

Medium weight Belgian linen (300 cm wide). This is a fine, good quality linen and because it is so wide it will go a long way. I use a backing fabric with this linen. International shipping available.

Alice Chinese silk threads – China

Website: http://stores.ebay.com/orientalcultures

Website: www.vendio.com/stores/orientalcultures

Email: orientalcultures@east-online.com

Alice speaks English and is always very willing to help with your individual needs. She sells over 800 shades of colour in pure Chinese silk. This is the real thing and can be subdivided into ultra-fine strands.

Eterna Silk – USA

Website: www.eternasilk.com

Email: online email form

The online shop is Yodamo.Inc. They stock a large range of affordable Chinese silk thread and ship worldwide.

Siesta Frames – UK

Website: www.siestaframes.com

Email: online contact form.

Siesta bar frames – these are the most lightweight, versatile frames on the market. They come in different sizes or mixed packs so that you can make up your own size.

Madeira – Australia

Website: www.sewingcraft.com

SSS Pty Limited
16-18 Valediction Rd
Kings Park
NSW 2148 Australia
Tel: 61 2 9672 3888

Ristal Threads – Australia

Email: info@ristalthreads.com

4 Hercules St
Murrumbateman
NSW 2582 Australia
Tel: 61 2 6226 8200